YOU ARE | FIGHTING FANTASY | THE HERO

THE
WARLOCK
OF FIRETOP
MOUNTAIN

STEVE JACKSON & IAN LIVINGSTONE

Fighting Fantasy: dare you play them all?

And look out for more books to come!

THE
WARLOCK
OF FIRETOP
MOUNTAIN

STEVE JACKSON
& IAN LIVINGSTONE

SCHOLASTIC

MOUNTAINS

Fang

RIVER KOK

LAINS

Stonebridge Anvil

Firetop Mountain

Zengis

KAY-PONG

DARKWOOD FOREST

Yaztromo's Tower

MOONSTONE HILLS

Deedle Water

FOREST OF SPIDERS

IVER

Largo

SILVER RIVER CHALICE

SILVERTON

Coven

Knotoak Wood

TROLLTOOTH PASS

ATER RIVER

WINDWARD PLAIN

FOREST OF YORE

VALE OF WILLOW

SALAMONS

TO THE FLATLANDS

LAIN

Shazâar

Black Tower

Vatos

CRAGGEN HEIGHTS

LEO HARTAS

Scholastic Children's Books
An imprint of Scholastic Ltd
Euston House, 24 Eversholt Street, London, NW1 1DB, UK
Registered office: Westfield Road, Southam, Warwickshire, CV47 0RA
SCHOLASTIC and associated logos are trademarks and/or
registered trademarks of Scholastic Inc.

First published in the UK by Penguin Group, 1982
This edition published in the UK by Scholastic Ltd, 2017

Trade ISBN 978 1407 18130 1
C&F ISBN 978 1407 18425 8

A CIP catalogue record for this book
is available from the British Library.

Printed by CPI Group (UK) Ltd, Croydon, CR0 4YY
Papers used by Scholastic Children's Books are made
from wood grown in sustainable forests.

1 3 5 7 9 10 8 6 4 2

www.scholastic.co.uk

CONTENTS

HOW WILL YOU START
YOUR ADVENTURE?

The book you hold in your hands is a gateway to another world – a world of dark magic, terrifying monsters, brooding castles, treacherous dungeons and untold danger, where a noble few defend against the myriad schemes of the forces of evil. Welcome to the world of **FIGHTING FANTASY!**

You are about to embark upon a thrilling fantasy adventure in which **YOU** are the hero! **YOU** decide which route to take, which dangers to risk and which creatures to fight. But be warned – it will also be **YOU** who has to live or die by the consequences of your actions.

Take heed, for success is by no means certain, and you may well fail in your mission on your first attempt. But have no fear, for with experience, skill and luck, each new attempt should bring you a step closer to your ultimate goal.

Prepare yourself, for when you turn the page you will enter an exciting, perilous **FIGHTING FANTASY** adventure where every choice is yours to make, an adventure in which **YOU ARE THE HERO!**

How would you like to begin your adventure?

IF YOU ARE NEW TO FIGHTING FANTASY...

It's a good idea to read through the rules which appear on pages 198-203 before you start.

IF YOU HAVE PLAYED FIGHTING FANTASY BEFORE...

You'll realize that to have any chance of success, you will need to discover your hero's attributes. You can create your own character by following the instructions on pages 198–199. Don't forget to enter your character's details on the Adventure Sheet which appears on page 206.

ALTERNATIVE DICE

If you do not have a pair of dice handy, dice rolls are printed throughout the book at the bottom of the pages. Flicking rapidly through the book and stopping on a page will give you a random dice roll. If you need to 'roll' only one die, read only the first printed die; if two, total the two dice symbols.

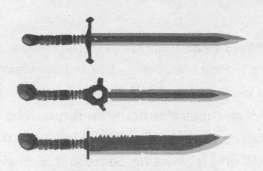

BACKGROUND

Only a foolhardy adventurer would embark upon such a perilous quest without first finding out as much as possible about the mountain and its treasures. Before your arrival at the foot of Firetop Mountain, you spent several days with the townsfolk of a local village some two days' journey from the base. Being a likeable sort of person, you found it easy to get on with the local peasants. Although they told many stories about the mysterious Warlock's sanctuary, you could not feel sure that all – or indeed any – of these were based on fact. The villagers had seen many adventurers pass through on their way to the mountain, but very few ever returned. The journey ahead was extremely dangerous, that you knew for certain. Of those who returned to the village, none contemplated going back to Firetop Mountain.

There seemed to be some truth in the rumour that the Warlock's treasure was stored in a magnificent chest with two locks, and the keys to these locks were guarded by various creatures within the dungeons. The Warlock himself was a sorcerer of great power. Some described him as old, others as young. Some said his power came from an enchanted deck of cards, others from the silky black gloves that he wore. The entrance to the mountain was guarded by a pack of warty-faced Goblins, stupid creatures, fond of their food and drink. Towards the inner chambers, the creatures became more fearsome. To reach the inner chambers you would have to cross a river. The ferry service was regular, but the ferryman enjoyed a good barter, so you should save a Gold Piece for the trip. The locals also encouraged you to keep a good map of your wanderings, for without a map you would end up hopelessly lost within the mountain.

When it finally came to your day of leaving, the whole village turned out to wish you a safe journey. Tears came to the eyes of many of the women, young and old alike. You couldn't help wondering whether they were tears of sorrow shed by eyes which would never see you alive again . . .

YOUR
ADVENTURE
AWAITS!

MAY YOUR STAMINA NEVER FAIL!

NOW TURN OVER...

Across the clearing is a dark cave entrance

1

At last your two-day hike is over. You unsheathe your sword, lay it on the ground and sigh with relief as you lower yourself down on to the mossy rocks to sit for a moment's rest. You stretch, rub your eyes and finally look up at Firetop Mountain.

The very mountain itself looks menacing. The steep face in front of you looks to have been savaged by the claws of some gargantuan beast. Sharp rocky crags jut out at unnatural angles. At the top of the mountain you can see the eerie red colouring – probably some strange vegetation – which has given the mountain its name. Perhaps no one will ever know exactly what grows up there, as climbing the peak must surely be impossible.

Your quest lies ahead of you. Across the clearing is a dark cave entrance. You pick up your sword, get to your feet and consider what dangers may lie ahead of you. But with determination, you thrust the sword home into its scabbard and approach the cave.

You peer into the gloom to see dark, slimy walls with pools of water on the stone floor in front of you. The air is cold and dank. You light your lantern and step warily into the blackness. Cobwebs brush your face and you hear the scurrying of tiny feet: rats, most likely. You set off into the cave. After a few yards you arrive at a junction. Will you turn west (turn to **71**) or east (turn to **278**)?

2

Test your Luck. If you are Lucky, you escape without attracting the Ogre's attention. If you are Unlucky, you curse as you kick a small stone which goes skidding across the cavern floor. You draw your sword in case the Ogre has heard it – turn to **16**. If you were Lucky, you creep down the corridor back to the crossroads. Turn to **269**.

3

The bell gives a dull clang and after a few moments you see a withered old man climb into a small rowing boat moored on the north bank. He rows slowly across to you, moors the boat and limps towards you. He asks you for 3 Gold Pieces. When you protest at the price he mumbles some flimsy excuse about 'inflation'. He begins to get angry at your protestations. Do you pay him the 3 Gold Pieces (turn to **272**) or threaten him (turn to **127**)?

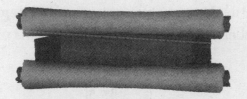

4

You find yourself in a north-south corridor. To the north the passage turns east some metres ahead. To investigate, turn to **46**. To the south, the passageway also turns east. Turn to **332** to go south.

5

A rough timber doorway is on the east wall of the passage. You listen at the door and can hear a jolly sort of humming sound. Do you want to knock on the door and go in (turn to **97**) or will you continue northwards (turn to **292**)?

6

The large solid door has no handle. You charge it, but to no avail. The door is not going to budge. You decide to give up and go through the opening you passed in the east-west passageway some way back. Turn to **89**.

7

You are on the north bank of a fast-flowing river in a large underground cavern. Turn to **214**.

8

The passage ahead ends at a sturdy door. You listen but hear nothing. You try the handle, it turns, and you enter the room. As you look around you hear a loud cry from behind you and swing round to see a wild man leaping towards you wielding a large battle axe. He is a mad BARBARIAN and you must fight him!

BARBARIAN	*SKILL 7*	*STAMINA 6*

There is a door in the north wall opposite, through which you may *Escape* during the battle (turn to **189**). If you defeat the Barbarian, turn to **273**.

9

Amazed at the success of your bluff, you decide to push your luck a little further. You can either examine the Skeletons' tools or pretend you're looking for work-sheets and look through the drawers of the various benches. If you choose the tools, turn to **34**. If you search the drawers, turn to **322**. You hear a noise from behind the north door and realize you will have to hurry!

10

You arrive back at the junction and turn northwards. Turn to **77**.

11

You follow the passage westwards until it turns round a corner to the south. Just before the bend is a signpost which reads 'Under Construction'. In front of you is the beginning of a stairway leading downwards. Only three steps have been built so far. A number of shovels, picks and other tools were lying on the ground by the steps but, as you turned the corner, they suddenly flurried into action and began working on the steps. You are now watching various tools digging and hammering as if being handled by invisible workers. A humming chant becomes louder and you recognize it as: 'Heigh-ho, Heigh-ho, It's off to work we go . . .' As you stand watching you start to chuckle – the scene is quite amusing. You sit and watch and even manage to chat to some of the magical tools. Gain 2 *STAMINA* points and 1 *SKILL* point whilst you relax. Then turn back up the passageway to the crossroads where you may go either northwards (turn to **366**) or southwards (turn to **250**).

12

As you pull the knob, a deafening clanging noise rings through the passageways. You frantically push the knob back to stop the alarm, but it has already had its effect. You can hear footsteps coming closer down the corridor. Turn to **161** to find what you have attracted. Note down the number **12** so that you may return to this section after fighting your battle.

When you have defeated this creature, you may either return to the junction (turn to **256**) or you may push the knob (turn to **364**).

13

Your head hurts and you feel dizzy as you rise to your feet. The four men stir into action and move towards you in single file with their weapons ready. You grope your way down the wall for the south door but it will be touch and go whether you make it. Your foot slips on a loose pebble and you fall to the ground. Before you can regain your footing, the creatures are upon you. Turn to **282**.

14

There are no signs of any secret passages, but you suddenly hear footsteps coming towards you. To find out what is coming, turn to **161**. You must fight this creature.

If you defeat the monster, turn to **117**. Note this reference so you know where to return to.

15

As you sit on the bench and eat your food, you begin to feel deeply relaxed and the aches from your body seem to be soothing themselves away. This resting place is enchanted. You may restore 2 additional *STAMINA* points as well as the normal amount (but only if this does not exceed your *Initial STAMINA* score) and restore 1 *SKILL* point if any have been lost. When you are ready to continue, move along the passage and turn to **367**.

16

You draw your sword, and as you do so the Ogre hears you and prepares to attack:

OGRE   SKILL 8   STAMINA 10

If you defeat him, turn to **50**. After the second Attack Round, you may *Escape* down the passage (turn to **269**).

17

Using the wooden stake and mallet (or makeshift mallet if you aren't carrying one), you form a cross and move towards the Vampire, backing it into a corner. It hisses and snatches at you but cannot come near you. However, it is going to be tricky getting the stake through its heart.

As you advance, you stumble and fall forwards. As luck would have it, the stake flies forward and plunges into the shrieking creature. *Test your Luck.* If you are Lucky, the stake pierces the Vampire's heart. If you are Unlucky, the Vampire is merely grazed by the wound (deduct 3 points from its *STAMINA)* and it flings you backwards across the room towards the west door. To *Escape* through it, turn to **380**. To keep on fighting, turn to **144**. If you were Lucky and killed the Vampire, you may look for its treasure – turn to **327**.

18

You walk westwards along the passageway. After fifty metres or so, the way turns northwards. Two or three paces up the passage, you hear a crumbling beneath your feet and you try to leap back as the ground gives way. *Test your Luck.* If you are Lucky, you manage to leap quickly backwards before a pit opens. If you are Unlucky, you are too slow and you fall over two metres down into a pit – lose 1 *STAMINA* point. If you were Lucky, you had better return to the junction (turn to **261**). If you were Unlucky, turn to **348**.

19

These two evil creatures are GOBLINS. They attack you one at a time.

	SKILL	STAMINA
First GOBLIN	5	5
Second GOBLIN	5	6

If you kill the Goblins, turn to **317**.

20

The skirmish commences. You have your sword, they have their axes. They come at you one at a time:

	SKILL	STAMINA
First DWARF	7	4
Second DWARF	6	6
Third DWARF	7	5
Fourth DWARF	7	5

If you win, turn to **376**. If the battle is going badly, you may *Escape* through the door. Turn to **291** – but don't forget your *Escaping* penalty.

21

The green blood of the dead Orcs smells foul as it seeps from their bodies. You step around the corpses and investigate the chest. It is a sturdy affair, made of strong oak and iron, and it is firmly locked. You may try to smash the lock with your sword (turn to **339**) or leave it alone and go through the open door (turn to **293**).

22

You poke around looking for signs of secret doors but can find none. You pause to ponder your situation and a small jet of gas hisses from the ceiling. You cough and choke to clear your lungs, but collapse to your knees. Your head spins and you flop to the floor in an unconscious heap. When you come to, you look around in an unfamiliar place. Turn to **4**.

23

The passageway ends in a solid doorway and you are surprised to see a leather skirt tacked along the bottom of the door. You listen but hear nothing. Will you enter the room (turn to **326**) or return to the junction (turn to **229**)?

24

After you have suffered your third wound, you notice that your strength is ebbing. Lose 1 *SKILL* point. You deduce that this is yet another magical power of this foul creature and you feel a shiver of panic. Will you continue or run? If you want to *Escape*, pay the penalty and turn to **360** to flee through the north door. Otherwise the fight goes on.

If you defeat the creature, turn to **135**. But from now on every third wound that the beast inflicts takes 1 point from your *SKILL*.

25

The paintings are portraits of men. Your spine shivers as you read the nameplate under the one on the west wall – it is that of Zagor, the Warlock whose treasure you are seeking. You look at his portrait and realize you are pitting yourself against an awesome adversary. You have the feeling that you are being watched and notice the piercing eyes following you as you move. You find yourself drawn towards his portrait and your fear rises. Lose 1 *SKILL* point. Do you have the courage to try to combat the Warlock? You may either leave through the north door straightaway (turn to **90**) – but treat this as an *Escape*. Or you may look through your pack for a weapon to use against the Warlock's power – turn to **340**.

You remember Di Maggio's small, leather-bound book, and silently mouth the spell contained within its pages.

You shout loudly at the Dragon and it stops in its tracks. It cocks its head to one side and eyes you suspiciously. You fling a stone at its head, and the rock bounces off its nose. The beast lets out an angry cry and breathes deeply, a roaring sound being created from within its throat. The Dragon exhales, and from between its teeth you can see another fireball building up. You prepare yourself, and as the ball of flame comes from its mouth, you cry:

'Ekil Erif
Ekam Erif
Erif Erif
Di Maggio'

The fireball continues no further. With an agonized scream, the Dragon tries to shake the flames from its snout. But there the burning continues.

Squealing in agony, the Dragon turns its back and leaps into the blackness, flailing its head from side to side. Turn to **371**.

27

The sword is enchanted and will aid you in battle. As long as you use this sword, you may increase your *Initial SKILL* by 2 points. You may also add 2 points to your current *SKILL* value. Add 2 points to your *LUCK* for finding this sword. Throw your old sword away and turn to **319**. If you would rather keep your own sword, leave your *SKILL* as it is and just take the *LUCK* bonus.

28

The mighty Giant lies dead! You search his cavern and find little of use, although a purse in his belt contains 8 Gold Pieces. You are a little concerned about the second chair; to whom does it belong? You decide to leave the cavern the way you came. Turn to **351**. But add 2 *LUCK* and 2 *SKILL* points for your victory.

29

Apart from the boots, which you decide to ignore, there appears to be little of value in the cavern. You decide to head back the way you came. Turn to **375**.

30

A loose stone falls out to reveal a rope in the rock. If you wish to pull it, turn to **67**. If you feel it would be wiser to leave it alone, you can return to the crossroads (turn to **267**).

31

If you have the jewel from the Eye of the Cyclops, you hold it in front of the Warlock. His intimidating stare turns to an expression of pain. He obviously feels the jewel's power. Suddenly his eyes turn white and his expression goes limp. Your confidence gains as you realize you have won your first real battle. Gain 2 *SKILL* points. Put the jewel into your pack and leave through the north door. Turn to **90**.

32

You toss the Cheese across the room at the Rats and they scramble for it, nipping and scratching each other as they fight for it. Having distracted them, you pass through the room and leave by the door in the north wall. Turn to **124**. Add 2 *LUCK* points for your good fortune.

33

The sleeping creature awakens startled. He jumps up and rushes at you, unarmed. With your sword you should be able to defeat him, but his sharp teeth look rather vicious. You may *Escape* through the door (turn to **320**) or stand and fight the ORC who is attacking you.

ORC   SKILL 6   STAMINA 4

If you defeat the creature, you may take the box. Turn to **147**

34

Looking through the tools you come across a mallet with a hardwood head and a chisel with a solid silver blade. You may keep either of these if you are prepared to forfeit one of the items of equipment you are carrying. If you wish to do so, make the appropriate adjustments to your Equipment List. The noise from the north door gets louder and you move up to investigate. Turn to **96**.

A wild-haired old man, clothed in rags, rushes at you screaming

35

As you step into the room, the door swings shut behind you. As it closes, there is a click and a hiss. From the centre of the ceiling, a jet of gas is filling the room with an acrid vapour. You breathe and cough deeply. You look at the door and then the key. Will you return to the door and escape quickly (turn to **136**) or hold your breath and dash for the key first (turn to **361**)?

36

The locked door bursts open and a nauseating stench hits your nostrils. Inside the room the floor is covered with bones, rotting vegetation and slime. A wild-haired old man, clothed in rags, rushes at you screaming. His beard is long and grey, and he is waving an old wooden chair-leg. Is he simply insane as he appears, or has this been some kind of trap? You may either shout at him to try to calm him down (turn to **263**) or draw your sword and attack him (turn to **353**).

37

Standing at the crossroads you may go either north (turn to **366**), west (turn to **11**) or south (turn to **277**).

38

You open the door to find the Werewolf's larder, a miscellaneous collection of bones and decaying meats. The smell is nauseating, although a jar of pickled eggs seems to offer fairly palatable food. If you wish to take these, there will be enough for two meals; add 2 points to your Provisions.

Back in the room you may now go out through the south door. Turn to **66**.

39

Your opponent is surprised as you disappear in front of him, but he raises his hands as if to cover his eyes and he scans the room with an intense glare. He can sense your presence but cannot make out exactly where you are. You draw your sword and advance. He tilts his head and sniffs the air. You will have to fight him from a distance as, if he gets his hands on you, your invisibility will be no advantage. But whilst you remain invisible, you have the following advantages:

- You may add 2 to your dice roll when determining your Attack Strength.
- Each successful attack will cause him 3 points of damage as, since he cannot see you, he cannot

defend himself properly.

- Each time he inflicts a wound on you, throw one die. If the number is odd, he wounds you as normal. If the number is 2 or 4, he only inflicts a 1-point wound. If you roll a 6, you can parry the blow and he does no damage.

Resolve the battle:

WARLOCK   *SKILL 11*   *STAMINA 18*

If you win, turn to **396**.

40

The ear-piercing sound gets louder and louder. The pain is unbearable. Reduce your *SKILL* score by 1 for the agony. You begin to grope in the dark for a wall. Do you head for:

The west wall? Turn to **355**
The north wall? Turn to **265**
The east wall? Turn to **181**

41

He is a powerful adversary – a WIGHT! He is large, strong and evil. The battle commences:

WIGHT   SKILL 9   STAMINA 6

You fight with your sword. After you have inflicted your first wound on him, turn to **310**.

42

You eventually arrive at the end of the passage, at a three-way junction. You may turn either to the west (turn to **257**) or to the east (turn to **113**).

43

You are in a north-south passageway. To go north, turn to **354**. To go south, turn to **52**.

44

Panting after the struggle, you sit down to collect yourself and finish the Provisions you started. Eventually you pack your bag and wade into the stream. Turn to **399**.

45

The Cheese hits the portrait and bounces off. You hear an evil laugh coming from the walls and realize the Warlock is mocking you. You decide to leave the room by the north door. Turn to **90**.

46

You are standing in a short east-west passageway, with a door blocking the way to the east. To the west, the passage turns southwards after several metres. To go round this bend turn to **4**. To go through the door, turn to **206**.

47

In the middle of the river, the bridge swings to and fro as it strains to take your weight. The handrail comes away suddenly as you lean on it. Roll one die. A roll of 6 sends you plunging into the river below – turn to **158**. A roll of 1–5 means you regain your balance. To go on, turn to **298**.

48

You are in an east-west corridor. If you go east, you will turn a corner northwards. To go this way, turn to **391**. To go west, turn to **60**.

49

The door squeaks open on rusty hinges. The room is dark and your eyes begin to adjust themselves as you close the door behind you. You hear a shuffling in the room but before you can react, a blow to your head knocks you senseless. Lose 2 *STAMINA* points and turn to **122**.

50

The slain creature crashes to the ground. You go through his garments and find nothing, but a small pouch hangs around his neck. Inside this pouch is a small bronze key, with the number 9 cast into it. You may take this if you wish. Nothing else is of value in the cavern so you leave and head back to the junction. Turn to **269**.

51

You drink the Potion and can see the look of astonishment spread across the Troll's face. He comes up to you and feels for you, but you step aside and he gropes the air fruitlessly. He thrashes around, clutching for you, but you are easily able to sidestep him. Eventually he gives up and returns to his chamber, just in time, as you feel yourself reappearing. Add 2 *LUCK* points. You may leave along the passage to the north. Turn to **287**.

52

You are standing at a T-junction where a passage to the east comes off a north-south corridor.

To go south	Turn to **391**
To check for secret passages on the way southwards	Turn to **362**
To go north	Turn to **354**
To check for secret passages on the way northwards	Turn to **234**
To go east	Turn to **291**

53

You charge the door, hitting it squarely with your shoulder. Roll 2 dice. If the number rolled is equal to or less than your *SKILL* score, the door opens (turn to **155**). If the number exceeds your *SKILL* score, the door shudders but does not budge, and you wince in pain as you hit the door – lose 1 *STAMINA* point and continue up the corridor (turn to **300**).

54

You are standing outside a door at the north end of a north-south passage. To go south, turn to **308**. To go through the door, turn to **179**.

55

Roll two dice. If the total rolled is less than or equal to your *LUCK* score *and* is also less than or equal to your *STAMINA* score, then you manage to hold on and manoeuvre the raft across to the north bank (do not deduct a *LUCK* point). You arrive safely but as you step on to the bank, the raft drifts away and makes its own way across the river to the south bank. Turn to **7**.

If you exceed your *LUCK* and/or *STAMINA* totals, the raft throws you into the water and you start to swim back to the south bank. Turn to **166**.

56

As your sword splashes into the water, a bubbly voice says, 'Thank you!' It now seems that the only way onwards is to swim downstream to the east. You plunge into the water. Turn to **399**.

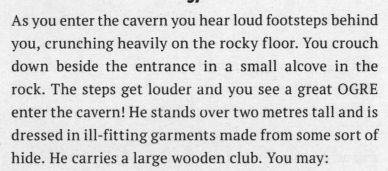

57

As you enter the cavern you hear loud footsteps behind you, crunching heavily on the rocky floor. You crouch down beside the entrance in a small alcove in the rock. The steps get louder and you see a great OGRE enter the cavern! He stands over two metres tall and is dressed in ill-fitting garments made from some sort of hide. He carries a large wooden club. You may:

Attack him as he enters	Turn to **16**
Try to creep out without him noticing you	Turn to **2**
Try to distract him by throwing something into a far corner of the cavern	Turn to **119**

58

Cautiously you creep along the passageway. After a short time it turns sharply to the north. At the corner there is a bench of solid wood and above the bench a sign reads 'Rest Ye Here Weary Traveller'. Here you may stop and eat Provisions if you wish (turn to **15**) or continue (turn to **367**).

59

You walk westwards for some time, then north round a peculiar bend which hairpins straight round to the south. Eventually you wind up at a three-way junction. Turn to **150**.

60

You walk along the corridor, only to find that the way westwards is blocked by a heavy portcullis. You walk back to where you were. Turn to **48**.

61

As you investigate the cavern, you suddenly hear a scurry of steps behind you and swing round to face the grotesque black shape of a GIANT SPIDER which has been stalking you. The Spider's body is at least a metre across and you quickly draw your sword to defend yourself.

GIANT SPIDER   *SKILL* 7   *STAMINA* 8

If you win the battle, turn to **29**. You may *Escape* from the fight down the passageway after two Attack Rounds and will end up at the junction – turn to **375**.

62

You continue along the passageway to the east. After some thirty metres it turns to the south. Following it round the bend you eventually come to a stop at a large armoured door. To try the door, turn to **6**. If you would prefer to return along the passage and go through the narrow opening, turn to **89**.

63

As you walk along the corridor, you can see ahead that it is getting narrower. At one point you stoop, and as you do so, a deep, resonating laugh starts up around you. Do you wish to continue? If so, turn to **281**. If you wish to turn back, turn to **10**.

64

The Ghoul dances with glee around your body, lays it next to the others on the ground, turns you over and sinks its teeth into your rump. It is not often it gets fresh meat to feed on.

Your adventure is over.

65

As you spring at the Chieftain, his servant rises to his feet, picks up a hefty wooden stick and joins the melee. But to your disappointment he attacks you! Ungrateful wretch! Seeing this, you may *Escape* through the door down the corridor (turn to **293**) or continue the fight (turn to **372**). If you choose to *Escape*, you suffer normal escaping penalties.

66

The door opens and you find yourself in the passage leading back to the riverbank. You return to the river and may now either go for the door in the middle of the rockface (turn to **104**) or go down the passage running off eastwards along the riverbank (turn to **99**).

67

You pull on the rope and a small door swings open revealing a passage into a north-south corridor. Will you return to the crossroads (turn to **267**) or go through the secret door (turn to **177**)?

68

The two GOBLIN torturers look at each other amazed, then look at you. They chatter to themselves and then indicate for you to wait while they go off and get another Dwarf to give them some more fun. They disappear out of the room and you cut down the Dwarf who is, as you guessed, quite dead. You decide it best to leave and press on northwards up the corridor. Turn to **303**.

69

Some way along the passage, the corridor bends round to the north and you follow it until you reach another junction. At this junction you see an arrow cut into the rock, pointing to the north, and you decide to try this direction. Turn to **244**.

70

You follow the cobbled corridor east, then north, then east again and finally north until you wind up at a crossroads. Turn to **267**.

A strange Goblin-like creature in leather armour asleep at his post

71

There is a right-hand turn to the north in the passage. Cautiously you approach a sentry post on the corner and, as you look in, you can see a strange Goblin-like creature in leather armour asleep at his post. You try to tiptoe past him. *Test your Luck*. If you are Lucky, he does not wake up and remains snoring loudly – turn to **301**. If you are Unlucky, you step with a crunch on some loose ground and his eyes flick open – turn to **248**.

72

You now have a fresh set of armour, equivalent to your own. Decide which of the two you wish to keep, throw the other away, and turn to **319**.

73

The passage ahead leads you northwards. The rocky floor becomes sandy until eventually you are walking on a sort of coarse sand. You notice the passage is widening and ahead you can hear a flowing river. You continue until you find yourself in a large cavern through which a river flows. Turn to **218**.

74

Test your Luck. If you are Lucky, you break his gaze and can prepare to attack. Turn to **279**. If you are Unlucky, you are under his control and drop your sword at his command – turn to **118**.

75

You sit back and rest from the exhausting battle. You may eat Provisions here. You prise the jewel from the still statue. It is heavy in your hand and is worth 50 Gold Pieces. You put it in your pack. As you explore the room and the statue, you notice that one of its breastplate sections is loose. When you open this, a small key is inside. You examine this and notice the number *111* on it. With a smile you put the jewel and the key in your pack and set off back to the junction. Turn to **93**, after adding 3 *LUCK* points – you have a valuable artefact here.

76

You arrive at another junction. An arrow on the wall points northwards and you decide to proceed in this direction. Turn to **244**.

77

Several metres up the passageway you arrive at a junction where you may turn either west or east. Set in the rock on the north wall is a small recess where you may rest and eat Provisions without being seen. If you wish to take Provisions here, do so. Afterwards you may set off either eastwards (turn to **345**) or westwards (turn to **18**).

78

The passage ends at a solid wooden door with metal hinges. Listening at the door, you hear strange mutterings and the clatter of what could be pots and pans. Whatever is in there, there are several of them. Do you want to go through the door (turn to **159**) or turn back (turn to **237**)?

79

The passageway ends in front of you in a dead end. If you wish to search for secret passageways, turn to **137**. If not, return to the crossroads at **267**.

80

The key fits the lock and opens the door. You find yourself in a large boathouse. Various boats, in different stages of construction, are lying around. Apart from the door behind you, there is another in the north wall. As you enter, the Skeletons stop their work and crane their bony necks around to look at you. They pick up planks of wood and hammers and advance towards you. There are five of them. Do you:

Smile nervously and back out of the door into the passage?	Turn to **129**
Tell them you've come about buying a boat?	Turn to **123**
Tell them you're their new boss and order them back to work?	Turn to **195**
Draw your sword and prepare for battle?	Turn to **140**

81

A noise startles you, prompting you to leave the room quickly. You walk up to investigate the north door. Turn to **205**.

82

The door opens to reveal a small, smelly room. In the centre of the room is a rickety wooden table on which stands a lit candle. Underneath the table is a small wooden box. Asleep on a straw mattress in the far corner of the room is a short, stocky creature with an ugly, warty face; the same sort of creature that you found asleep at the sentry post. He must be the guard for the night watch. You may either return to the corridor and press on northwards (turn to **208**) or creep into the room and try to take the box without waking the creature. If you want to try to steal the box, *Test your Luck*. If you are Lucky, he does not wake up – turn to **147**. If you are Unlucky, turn to **33**.

83

Test your Luck. If you are Lucky, you make it out through the north door – turn to **360**. If you are Unlucky, turn to **154**.

84

The door opens into a small room, comfortably furnished with a table, several chairs and a large bookcase which covers one wall. Seated at the table is an old man with a long grey beard, and squatting on the old man's shoulder is a small winged beast. This creature is no more than six centimetres tall. It has two arms and legs; its skin is a dusty grey colour. It has tiny sharp white teeth and its wings are folded behind its back. The old man says nothing as you walk in through the door, but he beckons you over to sit down at the table. He is tossing in his hand two small white objects. Will you:

Sit down as he tells you?	Turn to **204**
Leave the room and return to the junction?	Turn to **280**
Draw your sword and rush forward?	Turn to **377**

85

You are at a crossroads.

To go north	Turn to **106**
To go south	Turn to **373**
To go east	Turn to **318**
To go west	Turn to **59**

86

A huge jaw yawns open in front of you. By the size of it, the CROCODILE you are swimming towards must be at least three metres long. The beast slaps its tail in the water and glides towards you. You must fight two Attack Rounds.

CROCODILE   *SKILL 7*   *STAMINA 6*

Your combined thrashings attract a 'turbulence' in the water that you had noticed before and this now makes its way towards your part of the river. Out of the corner of your eye you notice this and must decide what to do. If you believe that the Crocodile is on its last legs and you wish to continue the battle, then do so. If you win, turn to **259**. Otherwise you can keep the beast occupied in the faint hope that this mysterious visitor will help you in some way. Have one more Attack Round and turn to **350**.

87

You arrive back at the junction and this time turn northwards. Turn to **262**.

88

You enter another small room, bare except for a fountain in the middle. Not a particularly grand affair, the fountain is a small carved fish, and a short jet of water comes from its mouth. A wooden sign hangs from the fish and this bears a message. It is written in Goblin tongue, at which you are not very proficient. The first word you cannot understand, but the others read: '. . . *NOT DRINK*'. But you are extremely thirsty. Will you drink from the fountain? If so, turn to **216**. Otherwise you can pass it by and leave through a door in the north wall (turn to **384**).

89

You climb through the opening and find yourself at the top of a narrow staircase leading downwards. Cautiously, you descend the stairs . . . Turn to **286**.

90

You open the door into a narrow passage and follow it northwards. Some metres up the passageway, it turns to the east, then turns to the north. However, at this second bend, there is a small alcove in the rock. It seems a convenient hiding place and a large rock forms a comfortable seat. You may stop here and eat Provisions if you wish. When you have rested, continue northwards. Turn to **253**.

91

If you are lucky, your cheating will not be discovered. *Test your Luck*. If you are Lucky, you get away with it. Roll two dice to see how many Gold Pieces you win. Mark these on your *Adventure Sheet* and turn to **131**.

If you are Unlucky, the four notice you are dealing from the bottom of the deck. They pick up axes from behind their chairs and turn on you. Turn to **20**.

92

You arrive back at the junction in the passage. You look left to see the cave entrance in the dim distance but walk straight on. Turn to **71**.

93

You arrive back at the junction and this time you turn northwards. Turn to **8**.

94

You walk along a passageway that runs due south, then turns west. After several metres, it ends at a three-way junction. You can check for secret passages along the way (turn to **260**) or go straight to the junction (turn to **329**).

95

You find nothing remarkable about the weapons, in fact not a single weapon looks more useful than your sword. As you search the debris, you hear a deep thumping from the north followed by a scream which sends a shiver down your spine. You rush to the north door to investigate. Turn to **205**.

96

The door opens into a short corridor about fifteen metres long. There are two doors, one at each end. You now realize what the noise was. More Skeletons! Four of them, armed with swords, are running down the corridor towards you.

They don't appear to have seen you and you notice a slight recess in the wall which may be a useful hiding place. You decide to try it. Turn to **374**.

97

A voice bids you 'Come in!' and you walk into a small room furnished with a table and chair, shelves, cupboards and the like, all of which have seen better days. Plates, bowls, cups and hundreds of old books line the shelves. In the midst of all this clutter, you see a little old man in a grubby white gown swaying to and fro in a rocking chair, still humming happily to himself, his eyes fixed on you, but seeming at peace with the world. He bids you 'Good day.' Do you:

Start to make conversation
with him?   Turn to **334**
Draw your sword and
charge at him?   Turn to **247**
Decide not to waste time with him
and leave, going northwards?   Turn to **292**

98

As you crawl into the room, a voice booms out: 'Welcome, adventurer. I have been expecting you.' You stop, look around and rise to your feet. The little old man has changed. He is not so old and grey any more, and he's of an imposing height. His eyes are deep and black and they are fixed on you relentlessly. Turn to **358**.

99

The passageway runs eastwards. Ahead of you, you can see that a solid-looking door blocks the passage. You step up to investigate. Turn to **383**.

100

Hesitantly, they agree to let you join in. As you play and chat, they loosen up and eventually you are all laughing and exchanging stories.

They seem quite harmless. You may play cards either fairly or you may try to cheat. If you wish to play fairly, turn to **346**. If you wish to cheat, turn to **91**.

101

Your lucky throw catches the Vampire unawares and he shrieks in agony as the stake sinks into his heart. You leap over and thrust it further into his body. His death cries grow weaker and his lifeless body slumps to the floor. Turn to **327**.

102

The door is not locked and opens. The room in front of you seems to be a small torture chamber, with various torture devices around the walls. In the centre of the room, two small, hunchbacked creatures are having their fiendish way with a Dwarf, who is tied to a hook in the ceiling by his wrists. The two hunchbacks are poking and cutting him viciously with their swords. The Dwarf lets out a final scream and falls silent, eyes closed. His captors make disappointed noises and look round angrily at you as if it were your fault that the Dwarf has collapsed. You must act quickly. Will you:

Close the door quickly and
continue up the corridor?   Turn to **303**
Draw your sword and try to
fight the creatures?   Turn to **19**
Stride over to the Dwarf, give him a
jab with your sword and put on an
evil laugh for the torturers?   Turn to **68**

103

You feel a stone move and behind it you find a lever. Will you pull the lever, or leave it and return to the crossroads? If you dare pull the lever, turn to **252**. If you go back to the crossroads, turn to **359**.

104

You find yourself in a short, narrow passageway with a door ahead to the north. You try this door. Turn to **49**.

A large Dragon stalking out of the darkness towards you

105

You rummage through your haversack. What is in there? You may attempt to use any of the following items if you have them on your Equipment List:

Potion of Invisibility	Turn to **39**
The Eye of the Cyclops	Turn to **382**
A piece of Cheese	Turn to **368**
Bow with Silver Arrow	Turn to **194**
A Y-shaped Stick	Turn to **215**

106

The passageway ahead runs northwards for some time. You may rest along the passage to eat Provisions. It then bends to the west and begins to get quite narrow. You reach a small rocky arch which you will have to stoop to get through. On the other side of the arch you pause and look around. You are in a large cavern which disappears into distant blackness. The cavern is partially lit by natural light which streams in through a hole in the roof. You cannot see a way through.

As you shine your lantern around the cavern, you hear a rumble. A dull glow flickers in the blackness. Suddenly, a jet of fire shoots from the depths of the cavern, narrowly missing you and singeing the mossy growths on the wall!

You throw yourself on to the ground and look up to see a large DRAGON stalking out of the darkness towards you. Smoke curls from its nostrils. Its scaly red skin glistens with an oily covering. The beast is some fifteen metres long! How will you attack the creature?

Draw your sword and
prepare to attack?   Turn to **152**
Search your memory for
another means of attack?   Turn to **126**

107

You tiptoe through the room, up a narrow staircase, ending up at the top of the stairs in a passage. 'That was easy,' you think, and you begin to have second thoughts about whether it would have been worthwhile to search the bodies. If you want to return and search the bodies, starting with the third, turn to **148**. If you want to press on, turn to **197**.

108

The moment your foot touches a hand tile, you feel a vice-like grip on your ankle and look down to see a ghostly white hand gripping your leg. You fight for your balance and manage to regain it. But to your horror you see that, from every hand-shaped tile in the floor, a similar apparition has appeared, and the floor across to the door is now scattered with ghoulish hands, flexing and snatching in the air. You draw your sword and chop at the hand. Resolve this battle:

HAND   *SKILL 6*   *STAMINA 4*

If you win, turn to **185**.

109

The liquid is smooth and watery and, as you drink it, you begin to glow. You feel euphoric and a little drunk at the same time. Your confidence grows and your weariness disappears.

The bottle contains HOLY WATER, blessed by the Overpriest of Kaynlesh-Ma. It has restored your *STAMINA* almost to full strength. Increase your *STAMINA* to 2 points below your *Initial STAMINA* (if your *STAMINA* was already higher than this, leave it as it is – you are strong enough!). Add points to your current *SKILL* to take the total to 1 point under your *Initial SKILL.* You may add 4 *LUCK* points for making such a lucky find.

If you have already looked at the parchment, you may leave the room northwards (turn to **120**). If you have not, you may look at it (turn to **212**) or you may forget about it and go northwards anyway.

110

You are now 8 Gold Pieces richer. You also find another 2 Gold Pieces in his boot, hidden there for safety. Turn to **319**. Record the Gold on your *Adventure Sheet.*

111

He will not be pacified. As you shift uneasily around the room, he shouts a word at the dog. Turn to **249**.

112

You see nothing in the room likely to help you in your battle. Will you:

Draw your sword, grit your teeth and advance?	Turn to **142**
Search your rucksack for a weapon to use?	Turn to **105**

113

You arrive at another junction in the passage. You may either go northwards (turn to **285**) or continue eastwards (turn to **78**).

114

The passage goes south, then east and you eventually find yourself at a crossroads. Turn to **359**.

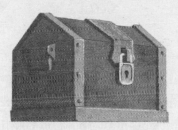

115

The poor wretches lying dead at your feet almost look happy to be relieved of the burden of life. But as you look down at them, you sense that you are not the only one to know of their deaths. Looking around the room, you may:

Investigate the weapons lying around	Turn to **95**
Go over to the dead body in the north-east corner	Turn to **313**
Check the barrels	Turn to **330**

116

The two drunken ORCS you now face are obviously startled at your entrance and, as quickly as they are able, they fumble around for the weapons. You must attack each one in turn. Their drunkenness allows you to add 1 point to your dice roll when rolling to work out your Attack Strength, during each Attack Round.

	SKILL	STAMINA
First ORC	5	4
Second ORC	5	5

If you win the battle, turn to **378**. If you wish to *Escape* during the battle, you may do so by turning to **42**.

117

You are in an east-west passageway. To go east, turn to **354**. To go west, turn to **308**.

118

As you approach he rises from his coffin, spreads his cloak and takes you under it. Your last living memory is a flash of pain as his sharp teeth sink into your neck. You should never have let yourself get into eye-contact with a VAMPIRE!

119

You open your pack and reach inside for something suitable to throw across the cavern. Check your Equipment List, choose one item to throw and cross it off your List. If you have no Equipment you will have to throw a Gold Piece. You throw the object across the cavern, where it lands with a clatter. The Ogre looks towards the noise, and goes over to investigate. Meanwhile you creep out, down the passage and back to the junction. Turn to **269**.

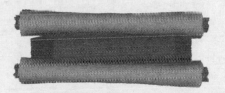

120

You leave the chamber, walk down a short passage and reach a staircase going up. You climb the stairs and arrive at the top in a passageway. Turn to **197**.

121

The corridor goes east for several metres, then south, then east again, where it finally ends. Will you investigate the dead end (turn to **103**) or return to the crossroads (turn to **359**)?

Standing motionless in the centre of the room are four men

122

You awake with a throbbing head and look around. The room is about eight metres square, with doors to the north and south. You have been dumped in the south-west corner. Standing motionless in the centre of the room are four men. At least, they *appear* to be men. Their skin is a greeny-grey colour. Their clothes are tattered and torn – and they are all staring vacantly at the ceiling. One carries a club, one a scythe, one an axe and one a pick. They are ignoring you completely.

Around the room are various peasant-style weapons (pitchforks, axe-handles, pointed sticks, etc.), one or two shields, and several barrels. In the north-east corner is a human corpse with a sword in one hand and a shield in the other. You move your hand up to your head to feel for signs of blood and you are relieved to find you are not bleeding. But as your hand moves, the strange creatures in the centre of the room turn their eyes down towards you. Do you:

Try to talk to them?	Turn to **268**
Jump to your feet and charge them with your sword?	Turn to **282**
Scramble for an exit through the south door?	Turn to **13**

123

Will they believe your story about buying a boat? Skeletons are pretty simple-minded, so roll one die. A 1, 2 or 3 means they believe you, and they all go running through the door in the north wall, leaving you alone in the Boat House. Add 2 *LUCK* points and turn to **184**.

A 4 or 5 means they're not sure. They send two of their members through the north door whilst the other three watch you with their makeshift weapons. Turn to **164**.

A roll of 6 means they definitely don't believe you and keep on advancing. Turn to **140**.

124

The door opens into a wide passageway and you follow this for some distance before reaching a junction. Here you may either go northwards (turn to **138**) or turn to the east (turn to **76**).

125

You pick up the rope. It looks normal. In fact it looks as if it might be quite useful. You open your pack to put it in. Suddenly, it comes alive in your fingers, snakes quickly up your arm and attempts to wrap itself around your neck. You struggle to cut the rope with your sword before its grip tightens. *Test your Luck.* If you are Lucky, you cut the rope and it drops to the ground. If you are not, the rope tightens – lose 1 *STAMINA* point. You must *Test your Luck* again to try to cut the rope, and keep trying until you do. Each time you fail, you lose another *STAMINA* point (and reduce your *LUCK* score). If you finally defeat the rope, you may leave through the north door. Turn to **73**.

126

Does the name 'Farrigo Di Maggio' mean anything to you? If not, you must fight the Dragon. Turn to **152**. If it does, turn to **26**.

127

He doesn't take at all kindly to your threats. As you argue and his anger builds, you notice a transformation taking place. He begins to straighten up and grows physically stronger in front of your very eyes. His face and arms grow hairy. His teeth become sharp and pointed. You must make a quick decision. Will you offer him 5 Gold Pieces to calm him down (deduct this from your Gold and turn to **272**), or prepare to attack him (turn to **188**)?

128

You hear a deep rumbling noise and the ground begins to shudder. Slowly and noisily the portcullis rises into the ceiling. You may now walk to the junction. Will you turn west (turn to **210**) or east (turn to **58**)?

129

You return to the riverbank and decide to try the door in the middle of the rockface. Turn to **104**.

130

The old man asks you your stake. You may bet between 1 and 20 Gold Pieces (but not more than you possess!). He tosses the white dice he has been playing with to you and asks you to roll. Roll two dice once for yourself and once for the old man. If your total is higher, you win the amount of your stake from the old man. If his total is higher, you lose your stake. You may continue for as long as you have Gold Pieces, and then leave through the door and return to the junction. Add 2 points to your *SKILL, STAMINA* and *LUCK* scores if you win. Turn to **280**.

131

You chat about various things and they seem eager to be friendly. They feel lonely in the dungeon with so much evil about and are happy to speak to visitors of a lawful disposition. They tell you that you are in The Maze of Zagor. The only way out is to go deeper into the dungeon. They tell you that the way through the maze is to leave the room, turn right, right, left, keep going straight . . . and then they begin to get a bit vague. They're not entirely sure it is correct.

You may, if you wish, eat a meal from your Provisions, but you will have to share it with them and thus will only gain half the normal *STAMINA* points. Eventually you thank them and leave the room. Go to **291**.

132

The shield is a standard wooden type. You may keep it or throw it away. Turn to **319**.

133

You are in a north–south corridor which ends in a dead end. You look around the rock face for signs of anything interesting, when suddenly a rock breaks loose above you and lands on your head. Although the blow was not particularly hard, you find you are feeling dizzy. You fight to remain conscious, but are unable to do so. You slump to the ground. When you open your eyes, you are at a junction. Turn to **52**.

134

The room is unoccupied and there seems to be no other means of exit. In the centre of the floor stands a table, and on this table are two helmets; one of bronze and one of iron. Both are about your size. Will you try one on, or is this worth the risk?

Try on the bronze helmet	Turn to **202**
Try on the iron helmet	Turn to **325**
Return to the junction	Turn to **87**

135

The Wight lies in a heap in the corner of the room. You approach his desk and open the box. There are 18 Gold Pieces within the box. You may take these with you – enter them on your *Adventure Sheet*. You can add 2 *LUCK* points for defeating the creature and may rest a while to take some Provisions. When you are ready, you may leave by the north door. Turn to **360**.

136

You arrive at the door, struggle with the lock and open the door. You burst out, closing the door behind you and take several deep breaths. Return to the junction (turn to **229**).

137

You find no secret passages, but as you press the wall, you hear a click. You feel dizzy and slump to the ground. When you come to, you do not recognize your surroundings. Turn to **354**.

138

The passage widens and you realize you are about to enter a large cavern. You can hear noises coming from the cavern ahead and you proceed cautiously. As you approach, you can make out a large figure in the distance and you are overawed as you realize that this oversized human must be at least three metres tall! Dressed in a leather tunic, the creature is absorbed in a meal he is eating at a table.

The cavern is at least a hundred metres across and must be the home of this GIANT. A large table and two chairs are along one of the walls, and it is here that the creature sits. Intent on his meal (a large pig), he is unlikely to notice you. Around the rest of the cavern you can see his straw mattress, a great furry pelt which may be his blanket or a shawl, and a huge stone-headed hammer, which you would have no hope of budging. A fire burns in one corner of the cavern, under a hole in the ceiling. There appears to be no other way through the cavern. Will you take on this brute (turn to **163**) or return to the junction (turn to **351**)?

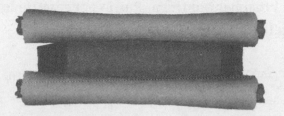

139

During your adventure, you will have come across various keys and should have collected some of these. You may now use three of these keys to try to open the locks on the chest.

Each key is identified with a number. To determine whether you have the right keys, add their three numbers together. Now turn to the section which has the same number as this total, where you will discover whether you have used the correct keys.

If you do not have three numbered keys, this is the end of your journey. You sit on the chest and weep as you realize that you will have to explore the mountain once more in order to find the keys.

The Skeletons advance and force you back to the door. The leader approaches, with two behind, and the final two behind them. Resolve the battle by first fighting the leader:

SKELETON   *SKILL 7*   *STAMINA 5*

and then fighting the pairs. Both members of a pair will have a separate attack on you in each Attack Round, but you must choose which of the two you will fight. Attack your chosen Skeleton as a normal battle. Against the other you will throw for your Attack Strength in the normal way, but you will not wound it if your Attack Strength is the greater, you must just count this as though you have defended against its blow. Of course if its Attack Strength is greater, it has wounded you in the normal way.

		SKILL	STAMINA
1st Pair:	SKELETON A	6	5
	SKELETON B	6	6
2nd Pair:	SKELETON A	5	6
	SKELETON B	5	5

If you win, turn to **395**.

141

When the old man learns of your quest for treasure he becomes angry and bids you begone – he'll have nothing to do with fortune-hunters. His dog senses his anger and snarls menacingly. You may either smile, thank him and exit through the south door (turn to **66**) or you may stay to try to pacify him (turn to **111**).

142

His booming voice calls out, 'Poor fool. Do you think you could match my power with your puny weapon?' You continue with determination. 'If it is a simple brawl you want, stranger, then I shall give you your last!' and with these words, he vanishes and reappears behind you. You swing round to face him and the fight starts. But this is a battle to the death. There is no escaping here.

WARLOCK   *SKILL 11*   *STAMINA 18*

If you win, turn to **396**.

A Giant Sandworm rears up and sways over in your direction

143

You squat on the sandy bank. As you prepare your meal you notice a movement in the sand a couple of metres to your left. The movement becomes quite turbulent and you spring to your feet, sword at the ready. Suddenly a large tubular head breaks through the surface, twists around in the air and picks up your scent. The smooth, segmented body of a GIANT SANDWORM rears up and sways over in your direction. As it does so, a large orifice, with short, spiky teeth, opens in what must be its head. You must do battle with this creature.

GIANT SANDWORM   SKILL 7   STAMINA 7

If you win, turn to **44**. If you want to *Escape*, after three Attack Rounds, you may dive into the river and swim downstream (turn to **399**), but you have lost the Provisions you started to eat.

144

The creature catches your eye with its own gaze and you find yourself unable to control your own actions. It beckons you forward. You move slowly towards it with your mouth gaping open. It tells you to throw down the stake. As you look down at the stake, you suddenly feel a surge of power return to your own will, and you fling the stake at him from close range.

Test your Luck. If you are Lucky, turn to **101**. If you are Unlucky, turn to **217**.

145

The box has fallen to the ground during your fight with the Snake and out of it has fallen a bronze-coloured key with the number 99 carved into it. You may take this key with you (note it on your Equipment List) and leave the room. Add 1 *LUCK* point and turn to **363**.

146

You find no secret passages. You return to the crossroads and proceed either northwards (turn to **366**) or westwards (turn to **11**).

147

You leave the room and open the box in the passage. Inside you find a single Piece of Gold and a small mouse, which must have been the creature's pet. You keep the coin and release the mouse, which scurries off down the passageway. Gain 2 *LUCK* points and turn to **208**.

148

As you search the body, you try to avoid looking at the terrible face, grey and decomposing. Maggots crawl from its nose and mouth. You jump back startled when its eyes suddenly flick open! Just in time you avoid a vicious slash from its long sharp fingernails. It quickly springs to its feet and eyes you with a sadistic leer spreading across its mouth. Turn to **230**.

149

As you watch the living mural, you are unaware of the speed with which your candle is burning. Suddenly it flickers and goes out! You again begin to hear the piercing screams and their pitch grows to an unbearable level. You drop to your knees clutching your ears and crawl towards the wall. Which wall will you crawl towards:

The east wall?	Turn to **181**
The north wall?	Turn to **265**
The west wall?	Turn to **355**

150

You are at a three-way junction.

To go north	Turn to **222**
To go east	Turn to **297**
To go south	Turn to **133**

151

You gain ground on the 'turbulence' in the water but a few metres from the north bank you notice two sinister reptilian eyes on the surface of the water watching you. You are swimming straight for them. If you decide you'd rather not face the owner of the eyes, you may turn round and head straight back to the south bank at full speed – you arrive exhausted, lose 1 *STAMINA* point and turn to **218**. Alternatively you can risk the eyes ahead – turn to **86**. You may try a detour which will send you nearer the 'turbulence' – turn to **158**.

152

Resolve your battle:

DRAGON   *SKILL 10*   *STAMINA 12*

If you win, turn to **371**.

153

As you put the two swords into your belt, your new one seems to take on a mind of its own. It cuts your leg (lose *1 STAMINA* point) and, as you draw it out, it turns rubbery in your hand. It's useless now so you fling it into the river. It seems that the only way forward is for you to swim eastwards down the river. You plunge in and start swimming. Turn to **399**.

154

As you move, the creature's eyes flash open. He sees you and slowly gets to his feet. His breathing becomes heavy and he stalks towards you. You must stand and fight him. Turn to **41**.

155

The door splits along its length and you can wrench the timbers apart to let yourself in. A torch hangs from one wall lighting up a small armoury room stocked with swords, shields, helmets, daggers, breastplates and the like. You examine the weaponry and find nothing appearing superior to your own sword. However, a circular iron shield with a golden crescent at its centre catches your eye. You pick it up and feel its weight on your arm. If you wish to take this shield it will aid you in battles by helping to fend off wound damage inflicted by a creature on you. If, in future during a battle in which you are using this shield, a creature wounds you, you may throw one die. If you throw a 6, the creature inflicts only 1 point of damage instead of the normal 2. If, for some reason, the creature would normally only inflict 1 point of damage, then a successful roll of 6 would mean that no damage is done. However, the shield is heavy and you will have to leave behind one item of equipment (adjust your Equipment List) to be able to carry it.

You now leave the room and continue up the corridor. Turn to **300**.

156

You charge the door with your shoulder. Roll two dice. If the number rolled is less than or equal to your *SKILL* score, you succeed – turn to **343**. If the number rolled is greater than your *SKILL,* you rub your bruised shoulder and decide against trying again. Turn to **92** to return to the junction.

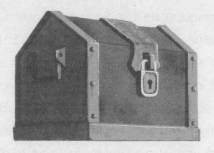

157

The door opens into an east-west passage, which turns north after several metres. To follow this direction, turn to **4**. If you decide against going through the door, turn to **329**.

158

The water around you bristles with activity, as if an invisible hand is dropping unseen pebbles into the river. You gulp – PIRANHAS! – and you begin to feel their sharp teeth biting into your flesh. You kick with your limbs and slash with your weapons to keep them off until you reach the south bank. Treat the Piranhas as a single creature.

PIRANHAS　　　　*SKILL 5*　　　　*STAMINA 5*

Resolve this battle.
If you win, you manage to scramble out of the water and lie panting on the south bank. You may eat Provisions here. Turn to **218**.

159

You open the door into a large room which can only be the dining room of the same warty-faced creatures you now recognize. Sitting round a large table are five ORCS busily drinking and dribbling their bowls of rat-gizzard soup. All are involved in a rowdy argument as to who will get to chew the rat bones left in the large soup cauldron, so they do not see you enter. You may be bold and prepare to attack them (turn to **365**) or you may not relish the prospect of taking on five of these creatures and try to escape. If you wish to leave the room, *Test*

your Luck. If you are Lucky, you get out without them noticing (turn to **237**) – there is no penalty for escaping. If you are Unlucky, they notice you. Prepare for battle and turn to **365**.

160

You follow a long, narrow passageway which goes south, then east, then south again until you eventually find yourself at a crossroads. Turn to **267**.

161

Make sure you have noted the reference as instructed on the last page! You will return to that reference after dealing with the creature you are about to encounter.

Your tappings and scrapings at the rock face as you search for secret doors and passageways resound through the dungeon corridors. Various creatures roam freely through the underworld and your noises have just attracted the attentions of one of the following monsters.

Roll one die. Consult the table below and over to find out what has come to investigate. Fight the creature as normal. Wandering monsters never carry any treasure. If you defeat this monster, return to the reference you have noted.

Die roll	Creature	SKILL	STAMINA
1	GOBLIN	5	3
2	ORC	6	3
3	GREMLIN	6	4
4	GIANT RAT	5	4
5	SKELETON	6	5
6	TROLL	8	4

162

The passageway ahead runs northwards and you follow this until you reach another junction. Here you may either continue northwards (turn to **23**) or you may turn westwards (turn to **69**).

163

You draw your sword and enter the cavern. The Giant stops in the middle of a mouthful, raises his head and sniffs the air. He swings round and catches sight of you approaching. Roaring loudly, he flings the pig's carcass at you. *Test your Luck*. If you are Lucky, it misses. If you are Unlucky, it hits you with quite some force – lose 1 *STAMINA* point. Then he picks up his hammer and prepares to club you with it. Resolve this battle.

GIANT　　　　　　*SKILL 8*　　　　　*STAMINA 9*

If you win, turn to **28**. You may *Escape* after three Attack Rounds down the passageway, where he will not be able to follow (turn to **351**).

164

You realize that the two Skeletons who have just run off will soon return and expose your bluff. You must react quickly. Will you beat a hasty retreat through the door behind you (turn to **129**) or draw your sword and lash out at the remaining Skeletons (turn to **236**)?

165

The old man thanks you and rather sheepishly ties up his boots. You explain that you mean no harm and he calms down, calling off his dog. He tells you that this area is the only passageway through to the inner chambers. Some years ago the river swelled after a particularly severe spring thaw and cut off supplies from the outside world. All the area's inhabitants starved to death but the Master, realizing he needed defences against the outside world, put a curse on the area. The last remaining creatures became the Undead and now guard the passageways through.

He starts to inquire about you. Will you:
Be straight with him and tell
him of your quest? Turn to **141**

Thank him for the chat and
leave through the south door?   Turn to **66**
Try to grab the keys and go for
the nearest door?   Turn to **249**

166

You land in the icy water and frantically swim for the south bank. To your amazement the raft turns round in mid-stream and makes its own way back to the south bank. You quicken your pace, aware that your splashings may at any time attract the attentions of any underwater creatures living in the river.

Roll one die. If you roll a 1, 2, 3 or 4 you make it safely back to the south bank. Turn to **218**. If you roll a 5 or 6, turn to **138**.

167

You find a secret door which opens into the bend where two passageways meet. To the north a short passage runs into a dead end, and to the east, the passageway reaches a crossroads. If you will step through this secret door into the passageway, turn to **187**. If you decide against going through the secret door, close it and return down the passage to the crossroads – turn to **359**.

A man-sized creature with a warty face, standing over a smaller creature

168

You open the door to a large room. A large chair behind a solid-looking table suggests to you that someone, or *something*, of rank uses this room. A chest in the centre catches your eye. In a corner of the room stands a man-sized creature with a warty face, standing over a smaller creature of similar race. With the whip in his hand, the ORC CHIEFTAIN has been beating his servant, who is whimpering beneath him. Will you:

Attack them both?	Turn to **372**
Spring at the Chieftain in the hope that his servant will aid you?	Turn to **65**
Leave the room and head back for the junction?	Turn to **293**

169

One by one all the keys click and turn in the locks. You have placed them all correctly! As the last key turns, the lid of the chest comes free and you open it. Turn to **400** to see what lies within.

170

The crucifix is solid silver and worth 4 Gold Pieces. Record this on your *Adventure Sheet* and turn to **319**.

171

You are standing at the north end of a short north-south passage. You are at a dead end. To investigate the wall, turn to **337**. To go southwards, turn to **187**.

172

The old man's eyes flutter open. He sees you and grabs for a half oar lying by his bench. You tell him you mean him no harm but he remains on guard and eyes you cautiously. Although he looks harmless enough, his dog could be dangerous. The man's boots are undone. Will you:

Rush the dog with your
weapon drawn?   Turn to **249**
Ask the man questions
regarding your quest?   Turn to **141**
Tell him his boots are undone?   Turn to **165**

173

Silver weapons only will be effective here. When the creature inflicts its *third* wound on you, turn to **24**. If you defeat it before this happens, turn to **135**, or you may *Escape* through the north door (turn to **360**). If you can use 'The Giver of Sleep', *Test your Luck*. If you are Lucky, you hit and the creature dies instantly. If you are Unlucky, you miss.

174

Turn to **198**.

175

You are standing in a narrow corridor. Behind you is a secret door to the east. Ahead of you is a crossroads. To go through the door, turn to **177**. To walk to the crossroads, turn to **267**.

176

As you walk up the passage, it visibly widens and eventually you find yourself standing at the mouth of a rough cavern, a natural cave in the rock. As you look into the darkness, the cavern appears to be about 30 metres deep, with no visible exit. Do you want to go into the cavern (turn to **270**) or go back to the junction (turn to **375**)?

177

You are standing in a north-south passage. To the north you can see a passage off to the east. To investigate, turn to **52**. To the south, the passage turns westwards. You may go to the southern end of the passage by turning to **391**. In the west wall in front of you is a secret door. To go through this, turn to **175**.

A strange-looking creature, half-man, half-bull

178

You tiptoe precariously across the room to the door in the north wall. You open the door and proceed through it. Turn to **162**.

179

You have entered a large square room. Broken pottery lies scattered all about. One large clay vase is untouched and is full of clear liquid. A large bowl is full of gold coins. As you enter the room the door slams behind you and you swing round to face a strange-looking creature, half man, half bull – who is glaring at you. He is a MINOTAUR, and he stalks towards you!

He lowers his head, horns pointing at your chest, and charges. You must fight him:

MINOTAUR   *SKILL 9*   *STAMINA 9*

After three Attack Rounds, you manoeuvre yourself round to be able to run through the door. If you wish to *Escape* at this time, turn to **54** and pay the penalty. If you continue fighting and kill him, turn to **258**. If you have already been in this room on this adventure and killed the Minotaur, you find it empty. Leave and turn to **54**.

180

The passageway goes west and then south. Finally you come to a stop at a dead end. You may return to the three-way junction and go east (turn to **70**) or north (turn to **329**), or you may investigate the dead end (turn to **22**).

181

You run along the wall searching for a door but find none. Your ears are on fire with the agony! Lose 1 *SKILL* point. You may try either the west wall (turn to **355**) or the north wall (turn to **265**), but you must find a way out soon!

182

Two of the keys fit the locks perfectly. The other doesn't. You leap to one side as a jet of clear liquid spurts from the chest. It just misses, but you lose 2 *STAMINA* points as the liquid emits an acidic vapour which makes you cough and choke.

You return to the chest and try another combination of three keys. Add the key totals and turn to that section.

If you have no more keys to try, you sit down exhausted and in despair after having got so near to your goal. Remember to look for keys next time you enter the dungeon!

183

You search the bodies of the dead Orcs but find only a few teeth, nails, bones and knives in their pockets. You search the cupboards around the room but find only crude bowls, plates and spoons. But under the serving hatch you find a thin leather case half a metre long. You may open the case (turn to **266**) or you may leave it behind and walk out of the door (turn to **237**). You are proud of your victory and may add 1 *SKILL* and 5 *STAMINA* points.

184

You are alone in the Boat House and have some time to search before the Skeletons will inevitably return. You may either search the drawers (turn to **322**) in the room, or may investigate the tools (turn to **34**) before they come back. As you begin to search you hear a noise from behind the door in the north wall.

185

The hand withers and shrinks back into the floor. At the same time, the other hands stop dead and slowly fade away downwards into the tiles. You decide this time to step on the star-shaped tiles, and step carefully across to the door in the north wall. The door opens. Add 2 *LUCK* points. Turn to **162**.

You try the handle and it turns

186

Turn to **198**.

187

You are standing in the corner of a bend in the passage. To the north the passage ends in a dead end. To investigate this, turn to **171**. To go eastwards, turn to **308**.

188

He now stands just under two metres tall. He advances towards you. His body is hairy. His teeth are pointed. His eyes flash. His fingernails are sharp claws. His nose has become a rat-like snout. He is a WERERAT!

WERERAT   *SKILL 8*   *STAMINA 5*

Resolve your battle with him. If you win, turn to **342**. If you decide to *Escape*, you may run over the rickety bridge (turn to **209**).

189

The door opens into a short corridor which ends several metres ahead at another door, similar to the one you have just come through. You listen and hear nothing. You try the handle and it turns, allowing you into another room of a similar size. But this room is splendidly decorated, with a polished marble floor and rough walls painted white. On each of the four walls hangs a painting, and there is another door in the north wall. You can either go straight through the room (turn to **90**) or you may stop to look at the paintings (turn to **25**).

190

You are in a narrow north–south corridor. There is a dead end to the north. You may check the dead end (turn to **167**) or give up and return to the crossroads (turn to **359**).

191

He shrieks and hides behind his desk. He is terrified of your aggressive manner. His squeaky little voice explains that he is the Mazemaster in charge of The Maze of Zagor. You talk to him and reassure him that you mean no harm and he eventually comes out from behind the desk. He sits down and as his confidence returns, a strange thing happens. His manner becomes firm and self-assured. He refers to a book, points his finger and the book slips from the shelf and floats on to the desk in front of him. You deduce that he is a Wizard of some power; perhaps even the dungeon Master himself, come to investigate you. You ask him the way out of the maze. He tells you to leave by the south door, walk past a door on your right until you can go no further and turn left. Go over a crossroads and turn left at the next one.

If you take his advice, leave through the south door and keep going until you reach the second crossroads	Turn to **308**
If you leave through the south door but intend to make your own way round	Turn to **392**
If you leave via the west door	Turn to **46**

Turn to **169**.

A large metal statue of a one-eyed creature

193

The door opens and you enter a small room. Your eyes widen as you look around to see that the walls of the room are covered in ornate stonework. Mosaics and marble inlays give this room a kind of beauty you have never seen before. In a corner of the room is a large metal statue of a one-eyed creature. In its single eye is a sparkling jewel. As there appear to be no other ways through the room, you will have to go back to the junction – but that large jewel is very tempting. Will you leave it alone and go back to the junction (turn to **93**) or try to take the jewel with you (turn to **338**)?

194

You load the bow and fire, but despair as the arrow flies through the air directly at him, stops centimetres from his chest and falls to the floor. He looks up and smiles at you with an evil, gloating smile. What can you do:

Draw your sword and advance?   Turn to **142**
Try something else from
your backpack?   Turn to **105**

195

This is a rather unlikely story, considering that they see very few humans around. Nevertheless, Skeletons are pretty dim – you knew this and that's why you tried the story. Roll one die. If you roll a 1 or 2, they don't believe you and keep on advancing. Turn to **140**.

A 3 or 4 means that they aren't sure, and send two of their number off through the north door whilst the rest hold you at bay with their weapons. Turn to **164**.

A roll of 5 or 6 means they've believed you and they all get back to work! Turn to **9**. Add 2 *LUCK* points.

196

You search the room. Try as you may you cannot find the secret switch to open the door in the bookshelf – the old man must have locked it from the inside. You do find 5 Gold Pieces in a drawer in the table. You decide to return to the junction to the south. Turn to **280**.

197

At the top of the stairs the passage turns sharply to the east. As you pause to get your bearings, you hear a creaking in the rock behind you. You spin round in time to see a heavy portcullis drop to seal off the passageway behind you. Your only way now is forward! You may either press on forward (turn to **48**) or may check the walls for secret passages (turn to **295**).

One of the keys turns, but the other two will not fit. As you struggle to try to make them turn, you hear two small clicks and then 'pings' as two miniature darts shoot from the chest at you. You leap backwards to try to avoid them, crack your head on the wall behind you, and slump to the floor, unconscious.

Test your Luck. If you are Lucky, the darts miss you, and you awake with a sore head. Lose 2 *STAMINA* points. If you are Unlucky, the darts strike and you never recover consciousness. If you *were* Lucky, you may try different keys (remember – *one* of the keys you just used fits perfectly). Add the key totals and turn to that page.

If you have tried all combinations for the keys that you have, you bury your head in your hands and weep after having got so far. You are so near to achieving your objective, but you will have to try again. Re-enter the dungeon – but remember to look for keys as you progress!

199

The passageway ahead widens and you can see ahead a large cavern. As you shine your lantern around it you can see crude stone weapons on the floor and a smouldering fire in the centre of the cave. But you see no way through. As you turn to make your way back you stop in your tracks to see two Neanderthal CAVEMEN barring your exit. They grunt aggressively at you. You draw your sword and must prepare to fight.

	SKILL	STAMINA
First CAVEMAN	7	6
Second CAVEMAN	6	4

Fight them one at a time. If you win, leave the cavern and return to the junction. Turn to **283**.

200

Turn to **387**.

201

You sink to the floor. You pull the dart out and decide to bandage the wound. This gives some relief, but you still feel weak. You decide to take it easy and examine the contents of the chest, but if you wish you may eat some Provisions here. There are 25 Gold Pieces and the label on the bottle shows it to be a Potion of Invisibility, good for one dose. The glove is a mystery. You may put any or all of these into your haversack and leave the room. Turn to **293**.

202

You place the helmet on your head. It fits well. Suddenly a searing pain flashes across your forehead. You cannot think straight. This helmet is cursed and, try as you might, you cannot remove it! Reduce your *SKILL* score by 1. The pain soon subsides, but you still cannot shift the helmet. You stagger back to the junction, trying desperately to compose yourself. Turn to **87**.

203

Add 1 point to your *LUCK* for defeating the Werewolf. You may rest and eat Provisions if you wish. As you look around the room there appears to be little of use, although the bunch of keys looks interesting, particularly the one marked 'Boat House'. None are numbered. You may take the keys if you wish. There are doors to the west and south. If you open the west door, go to **38**. If you want to go south, turn to **66**.

204

The old man does not look up from the table, but his devilish little pet eyes you suspiciously and starts chattering in a small squeaky voice. The old man grunts and asks you whether you are game for a wager. Will you accept (you may only do so if you have at least one Gold Piece with you)? If so, turn to **130**. If not, you may either leave the room (turn to **280**) or attack the man (turn to **377**).

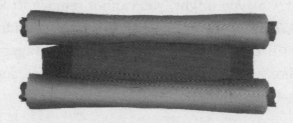

205

The door opens and you find yourself in a dark crypt of some kind. The room is very large. At one end is an altar, and various coffins are strewn about the room. There is a door behind you in the south wall, and also one in the west wall. If you want to investigate the room further, turn to **254**. If the place gives you the creeps, you can leave via the west door (turn to **380**).

206

You enter a large square room. In the centre of the room is a grey-haired old man sitting at a desk. His desk is covered in papers and parchments of various sorts and he holds a long quill pen. He is surrounded by books. Thousands of them line the shelves around the walls, from floor to ceiling. As you enter he looks up at you. Will he recognize you? If you have been in this room before, turn to **284**; if not, turn to **341**.

207

Going through the door you enter a large room. Various bits of wooden debris are strewn untidily across the floor. Apart from your entrance door, there is also a door in the north wall. In one corner is a crude wooden desk with a box on it. In another corner, apparently asleep (or dead), is a hideous-looking man-sized creature with warty skin, wild hair and long claws for fingernails. Will you tiptoe out through the north door (turn to **83**) or tiptoe across to the desk to look at the box (turn to **154**)?

208

Further up the passage along the west wall you see another door. You listen at it but hear nothing. If you want to try opening the door, turn to **397**. If you want to continue northwards, turn to **363**.

209

The timbers of the bridge are rotting and decayed from years of neglect. A single plank snaps under your foot. Roll one die. A roll of 6 sends you splashing into the river below – turn to **158**. A roll of 1–5 means you regain your footing. Turn to **47**.

210

Shortly along the passage you arrive at another junction where you may go either straight ahead westwards (turn to **225**) or northwards (turn to **357**).

211

Wights are vulnerable only to weapons made of solid silver. If the weapon you are using is not made of silver, have one more Attack Round. Remember that any wounds he inflicts on you will count, but your wounds will not harm him, and he will still be at full strength *(SKILL 9 STAMINA 6)* unless you have chosen a silver weapon.

If you have a silver weapon, you had better use it now and turn to **173**. If you have not, or if you have suffered enough damage, you'd better run for the north door – turn to **360**. Remember that you are *Escaping* here and he inflicts a final wound as you flee.

212

The parchment is well worn and almost illegible. It is a map of some sort, headed '*The Maze of Zagor*'. You can make little sense of it, although a room to the north is marked '... GER' and another to the east is marked 'SM ... P ... LE'.

You fold up the map and put it in your pocket. If you have not yet tested the liquid and wish to do so, turn to **369**. Otherwise, you can make your way northwards (turn to **120**).

213

The door is locked. You may try to charge it down by rolling two dice. If the number rolled is equal to or less than your *SKILL* score, the door bursts open – turn to **36**. If the number is greater than your *SKILL* score, the door remains locked, you lose 1 *STAMINA* point for your bruised shoulder and you must progress up the passage – turn to **314**.

214

Facing northwards, the rock face is smooth and glistening with moisture. Moss of many different hues grows on the surface. There is an eerie silence punctuated only by the splashings of the river as it flows behind you. You have three options:

A passage runs off to the north-
west. If you take this route   Turn to **271**

A large timber door is directly in
front of you in the middle of the
rock face. If you open the door   Turn to **104**

Another passage runs out along
the river eastwards. To follow this
along the riverbank   Turn to **99**

215

You reach into your pack for the stick only to find it split in two pieces! It has broken during your adventure. What else can you try:

Draw your sword and advance?   Turn to **142**

Try something else from
your pack?   Turn to **105**

216

The water is refreshing. As you drink more you feel a glow spreading through your body as if you were drinking at the fountain of life. Add 4 *STAMINA* points, and restore your *SKILL* and *LUCK* scores to their *Initial* levels. The fountain of life for you must be the fountain of death for the evil Goblins. You may eat Provisions here. When you have rested, leave through the north door. Turn to **384**.

217

The stake narrowly misses the Vampire's head. As you watch it travel, you pick up the creature's gaze again. He beckons you towards him once more. Your will has gone. Turn to **118**.

A rickety old bridge crosses on the right

218

You are on the south bank of an underground river facing across its black depths. There appear to be four ways of crossing. To your left, a rusted bell bears the sign: 'Ferry Service 2 Gold Pieces – Please Ring.' There is a small raft in front of you on the bank with a long stick resting beside it: you could punt across the river. A rickety old bridge crosses on the right. If you don't trust any of these, you may swim. Which will you choose?

Ring the bell	Turn to **3**
Punt the raft across	Turn to **386**
Risk the bridge	Turn to **209**
Swim	Turn to **316**

219

Turn to **182**.

220

He is enraged by your pleasantries. He waves his hand in the air, mumbles a few strange syllables and then points at you. You feel your head spinning and pass out. You awake in a dead-end passage. Turn to **171**.

221

What are these mysterious items you have collected?
Which have you written down first on your Equipment
List:

The armour?	Turn to **72**
The shield?	Turn to **132**
The sword?	Turn to **27**
The gold?	Turn to **110**
The crucifix?	Turn to **170**

222

You walk up a long corridor, round a sharp hairpin
bend at the top and finally along an east-west corridor,
eastwards to a crossroads. Turn to **85**.

223

The door is firmly locked. You may try to force it open

(turn to **53**) or you may continue along the corridor (turn to **300**).

224

As your eyes watch the creature's movements, they suddenly make contact with its piercing stare. You are mesmerized and, as it beckons you towards it, your will disappears. Turn to **118**.

225

The passageway continues westwards and then turns due north. Some way up, you reach a junction where a narrow passage runs off to the west. Will you continue northwards (turn to **77**) or take the west way (turn to **63**)?

226

You walk a short distance south and find yourself at a crossroads. Turn to **267**.

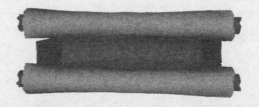

Sitting in the room around a wooden table are four tiny men

227

The door opens and you find yourself in a small, smoke-filled room. Sitting in the room around a wooden table are four tiny men, each about one metre tall, but all are apparently fully mature, with weathered skin and long, bushy beards. They are cursing, laughing and joking as they play a card game. Each one is leaning back on his tiny chair, puffing a long clay pipe. On the table are a number of copper coins and four mugs of ale.

As you walk in, their merriment stops. They are on their guard but don't appear to be too dangerous. One stands up and makes some comment about your lack of manners, not knocking before you came in. The others nod their agreement. Do you:

Chat to them and try to befriend them?	Turn to **131**
Apologize, bow and leave the room?	Turn to **291**
Offer to join in their card game?	Turn to **100**
Draw your sword and go for the leader?	Turn to **20**

If you have already been in this room, you find it empty. Turn to **291**.

228

You find no secret passageways. You are careful not to make too much noise in case you attract any wandering creatures. You stop and listen but cannot hear anything. You return to the crossroads. Turn to **85**.

229

You arrive back at the junction and this time turn right. Turn to **69**.

230

The creature now standing before you is a semi-decayed man. His quick eyes dart from side to side watching you. His long tongue flashes out with a hissing noise. His teeth and nails are sharp and he doesn't seem to be afraid of your weapon. He is a GHOUL!

GHOUL   *SKILL 8*   *STAMINA 7*

He has the ability to paralyse you if he scores four separate wounds on you during this battle, so beware! If you defeat him, turn to **390**. If he kills or paralyses you, turn to **64**.

231

Turn to **182**.

232

Almost exhausted after your awkward fight with the Spider, you set to work on hacking the boots off with your sword. Eventually they come free and you may leave the cavern down the passageway and back to the junction. Turn to **375**.

233

Turn to **198**.

234

You find no secret passages. However, your rummagings attract the attentions of something sinister ... Turn to **161** to discover what has appeared in the passageway in front of you. Fight this monster.

If you defeat the creature, you can continue up the passageway by turning to **43**. Write down '**43**' so you will know where to go.

235

You follow the passage westwards, then it turns sharply to the north and, some metres further on, a passage runs off to the west. If you would like to go along the westwards passage, turn to **176**. If you want to carry on northwards up the passage, turn to **5**.

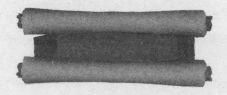

236

The battle commences. The Skeletons attack you one by one:

	SKILL	*STAMINA*
SKELETON A	6	5
SKELETON B	6	6
SKELETON C	5	5

If you win, turn to **395**.

237

You move swiftly down the passage and arrive back at the junction. Turn northwards this time – turn to **285**.

238

You are at a three-way junction.

To go east	Turn to **70**
To go west	Turn to **180**
To go north	Turn to **329**

239

You think back to the words of the old man. 'You might need it sooner than you think . . .' You grope in your pack and pull out the candle. Immediately it lights itself of its own accord. The howling stops and the room appears bathed in a blue light from the candle. On the walls, the figures in the mural are *moving*! They are mouthing silent screams as if trapped in a two-dimensional hell. On the wall opposite is another door, which you may leave through (turn to **88**), or you may stay to investigate (turn to **149**). Add 1 *LUCK* for your foresight.

240

The box is light, but something rattles within. You open the lid and a small SNAKE darts out to bite at your wrist! You must fight the Snake.

SNAKE   *SKILL 5*   *STAMINA 2*

If you kill the Snake, turn to **145**.

241

As you attack the portrait with the wooden stake, you feel a wrench of pain in your wrist. You are forced by some unseen power to drop the stake. You decide to run and leave through the north door. Turn to **90**, but lose 1 more *SKILL* point in awe of the Warlock's power.

242

The door opens to reveal a small, dimly lit room. The walls are hung with ornate curtains, laced in silver and gold. A single flame burns in one corner, throwing light on a low table in the middle of the floor. On this table is a large chest. You step up to investigate the chest and from all around, yet from nowhere, a mysterious sound fills the room. It sounds like the rumbling of thunder clouds preparing to make storm.

You approach the chest and can see that it is held shut by three locks. As you approach, the noise gets louder. Will you:

Hack at the box with your sword to try to split it open?	Turn to **379**
Search through your bags to see if you can find keys to fit?	Turn to **139**

243

To your horror, you realize that this dummy lever was a trap! Although it looked like a handle, it was in fact a wax-coated sword blade and it has now cut your hand badly. Did you use your right or your left hand?

Roll one die. If the number you roll is odd, this was your sword hand and your fighting prowess has been severely hampered. Lose 3 *SKILL* points and 1 *STAMINA*. If you rolled an even number, you used your other hand, and so the injury is not quite so important. Lose 1 *SKILL* point and 2 *STAMINA*. If you now wish to pull the right lever, turn to **128**. If you don't wish to pull the right lever, you won't be getting much further – and remember which hand you will use!

244

The passage runs northwards, and ahead you can hear the splashings of an underground river. The air becomes cool and fresh. You soon reach a wide opening of a river bank but despair as you look across to see no way through on the other side. To the east the river flows through a cave in the rock. You may either sit, rest and eat Provisions (turn to **143**) or continue by what seems to be the only way forward, jumping into the river and swimming downstream (turn to **399**).

245

Turn to **198**.

246

You set off south along a cobbled passageway. It swings west, then south, then west again until you find yourself at a three-way junction.

To go north	Turn to **329**
To go west	Turn to **180**
To go back east	Turn to **70**

247

He is a little startled by your onslaught, but simply raises his hand. As he does so, you suddenly collide heavily into ... apparently nothing. You sit on the floor in a heap, rubbing your nose. Lose 2 *STAMINA* points. The old man chuckles and says, 'You poor fool. Did you think I was defenceless in such a den of evil as this? You will regret your folly.' You rise to your feet and return to the passageway, turning north up the corridor. Turn to **292**.

248

The creature that has just awakened is an ORC! He scrambles to his feet and turns to grasp at a rope which is probably the alarm bell. You must attack him quickly.

ORC　　　　　*SKILL 6*　　　　　*STAMINA 5*

If you defeat him, you may continue up the passage – turn to **301**.

249

The dog springs as you move. Its hideous black teeth are coming straight for your throat! Two metres from you, a blast of fire shoots from its mouth right at your face! You duck just in time but must now fight the beast.

DOG　　　　　*SKILL 7*　　　　　*STAMINA 6*

In addition to its normal attack, throw one die every Attack Round for its fiery breath. On a roll of 1 or 2, it scorches you for 1 point of damage – subtract from your *STAMINA* – but on a roll of 3–6, you avoid the blast. You may use your *LUCK* against the fire. The only *Escape* open is through the south door (turn to **66**).

The old man watches the fight but does not move unless you kill his dog. If you kill the dog, you may *Escape* through the south door (turn to **66**), but you will not have time to take anything with you. If you wish to stay, turn to **304**. Add 1 *LUCK* point anyway.

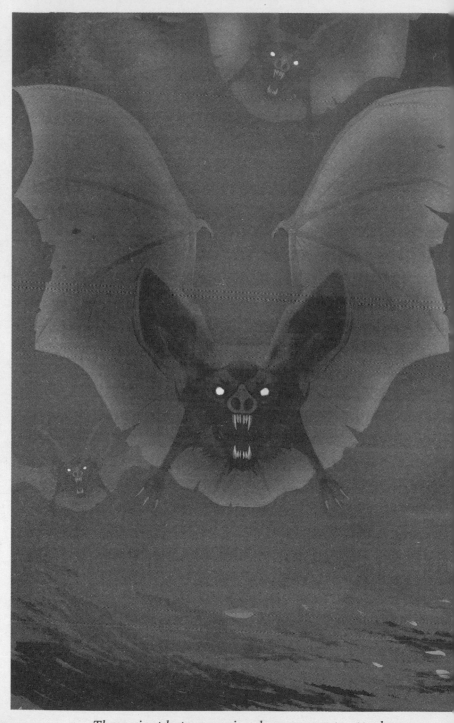

Three giant bats swooping down on you to attack

250

You are in a short passageway which comes to a dead end several metres ahead of you. You study the rock face carefully but there appears to be no way through. You return to the crossroads and this time continue straight ahead northwards. Turn to **366**.

251

The passageway twists sharply northwards and ahead you can hear water flowing. You eventually reach the south bank of an underground river. As you stand on the pebbled bank you hear a fluttering of wings and look up to see three GIANT BATS swooping down on you to attack. Fight these three as a single creature:

GIANT BATS   *SKILL 6*   *STAMINA 6*

If you win, turn to **344**. You may *Escape* by jumping into the river (turn to **399**).

252

You pull the lever and, with a great groaning noise, the rock face in front of you and the ground you are standing on start to move. As if you were on a giant rotating table, you spin round until you stand on the *other* side of a rock face in a north-south passage. Will you go north (turn to **312**) or south (turn to **226**)?

253

The passageway ends in another wooden door, this time a small one with a carved bone handle. You listen but hear nothing coming from inside. You try the handle and the door opens into a pear-shaped room with a rough stone floor, making walking across it somewhat awkward. In one corner of the room is a pile of rubble, mainly stones and dust, but there are also two odd-shaped pieces of wood and a length of rope. A door in the north wall leads on. Will you:

Examine the bits of wood?	Turn to **328**
Study the length of rope?	Turn to **125**
Leave through the north door?	Turn to **73**

254

The silence is deathly. A slow drip startles you as you creep around the coffins. The altar is ornately carved and studded with jewels. Beautifully woven drapes hang from the walls although they are threadbare in places. There are three coffins in the room. A creaking noise makes you whirl round and the light from your lantern falls on the largest coffin. It is opening!

As you watch, a tall man with a white face sits upright. His eyes open and fall on you. His expression changes from one of tranquillity to one of abject hate. His mouth opens and a terrifying hiss comes from his throat. His teeth are wolf-like. He beckons you to come over. Do you:

Approach him as he wishes?	Turn to **352**
Draw your sword and prepare to fight?	Turn to **333**
Reach into your bag for another means of attack?	Turn to **279**
Run for the west door?	Turn to **380**

255

The passageway ends in a sturdy wooden door. If you want to try opening it, turn to **193**. If you want to go back to the junction and try another route, turn to **93**.

256

You are at a junction where you may go north (turn to **398**), although this passage ends shortly in a dead end. You may go west (turn to **297**) or you may go south (turn to **114**).

257

The passageway runs straight for several metres and then ends at a wooden door. You listen at the door and hear angry shouting coming from within. Will you investigate (turn to **168**) or turn back (turn to **293**)?

258

You sort through the broken pots and find little of interest. The liquid looks, smells and tastes like water. The coins in the pot are a fraud. Eight genuine Gold Pieces lie on the surface of the pile (and you may take these) but underneath are merely painted pieces of pot.

As you tip the vase out it slips and breaks. A red-coloured key appears, hidden inside a false bottom in the bowl. You may take this key. It is inscribed with the number *111*.

You may rest here and eat some Provisions. You may add 2 *LUCK* points for defeating the Minotaur. Finally you leave the room. Turn to **54**.

259

As you swim to the bank away from the Crocodile you look back to see the mysterious 'turbulence' approach the reptile's body, break into a frenzy and then move off, leaving not a trace of the animal. Thankful that you were not there to find out what it was, you lift yourself out of the water on to the north bank. Add 1 *SKILL* and 2 *LUCK* points. Turn to **7**.

260

You find no secret passages. If you are on your way north, turn to **359**. If you are going south, turn to **329**.

261

You reach the junction and continue eastwards. Turn to **345**.

262

Some way up the passage, you reach another junction where you may either go eastwards (turn to **199**) or turn westwards (turn to **251**).

263

You shout: 'You are freed, old man!' at the top of your
voice. Instantly, his rantings cease. He stops dead in
his tracks and sinks to the floor, weeping loudly. As
he gradually composes himself, he thanks you many
times. You talk with him in the hope of discovering
some of the secrets of the mountain and he begins to
tell his story. Many years ago he was an adventurer
like you in search of the Warlock's treasure. He was
captured by the Orcs and thrown into his solitary cell
as a sort of pet for the creatures. You ask whether he
would like to accompany you into the mountain, but he
simply wants to leave and see the world again. You ask
him for advice but he says he knows little. He advises
you to pay your respects to the boatman. He tells you
that you must pull the right-hand lever on the wall
ahead to open the iron gate at the end of the passage.
He has also learned that the keys to the Boat House
are guarded by a man and his dog. You shake hands,
leave the room and go your separate ways. Add 1 *LUCK*.
Turn to **314**.

264

There is no way you are going to charge the door down, as it is twelve centimetres of solid oak! You bruise your sword arm at the attempt – lose 1 *SKILL* point. You can only get through the door if you have the Boat House key (if you have this key, turn to **80**, and more fool you for not using it straightaway). Otherwise you will have to return to the riverbank and try again. Turn to **129**.

265

You grope around the length of the wall and find a door. Quickly you fumble with the handle. It opens! Turn to **88**.

...THE GIVER OF SLEEP TO
THOSE WHO NEVER CAN...

The case opens easily

266

The case opens easily and inside you find a magnificent bow and one silver arrow. An inscription on the case says: 'The giver of sleep to those who never can'. You put the bow, arrow and case in your pack and leave the room, but you may eat Provisions first – and add 1 *LUCK* point. Turn to **237**.

267

You now stand at a crossroads.

To go north	Turn to **312**
To go south	Turn to **246**
To go west	Turn to **79**
To go east	Turn to **349**

268

Their vocabulary is limited to a series of moans and groans. They appear not to be intelligent at all. Furthermore your conversation merely serves to attract their attention to you. They grip their weapons and it looks as though you will have to fight them. However, there is a slim chance that you could make it to the door you came in through. If you want to try for that door, turn to **13**. If you have resigned yourself to a battle, turn to **282**.

269

You arrive back at the junction and turn westwards. Turn to **225**.

270

You enter the cavern and look around to see dozens of beautifully coloured stalactites and stalagmites bordering the perimeter. Numerous drips can be heard, but the whole place seems like a magic grotto. Near the back of the cavern, you come across a pair of boots, which seem to have been made quite recently. Will you:

Continue investigating
the cavern?   Turn to **61**
Try on the boots?   Turn to **394**
Leave the cavern and return
to the junction?   Turn to **375**

271

The short passage begins to narrow and ends a few metres ahead at a doorway. If you wish to go through the door, turn to **336**. If you decide against this direction and go back to the river, turn to **214**.

272

He calms down, takes the Gold (deduct this from your Gold)

and rows you across to the north bank. After mooring the boat he ambles off down a passageway. Turn to **7**.

273

A search of the room reveals nothing of any value, although an old box in the corner contains a wooden mallet and five short stumps of wood, sharpened at one end. You may take these if you wish, and can now leave through the door in the north wall. Turn to **189**.

274

You leave the cavern along a long, narrow corridor. After several hundred metres, it ends at a large wooden door which is slightly ajar. Carefully you ease it open a little further and poke your head around the side to see what is in the room. You see a small old man sitting at a table on his own, playing with a pack of cards. He looks quite a harmless old soul, grey-haired and bearded. He is seated. What will you do:

Burst through the door, sword drawn,
to surprise the old man? Turn to **324**
Knock on the door and enter, greeting
the old man courteously? Turn to **356**
Get down on all fours and try to creep
into the room unnoticed? Turn to **98**

Its eyes flick open

275

As you move over towards the second body, you accidentally kick the third corpse on the floor. Its eyes flick open and it quickly sits up and slashes at you with its long, sharp fingernails.

Test your Luck. If you are Lucky, the creature misses. If you are Unlucky, it has caught you across the leg and you suffer 1 *STAMINA* point's worth of damage. Turn to **230**.

276

Turn to **182**.

277

You are in a short passageway which comes to a dead end several metres ahead of you. You may search for secret passages (turn to **146**), or you may return to the crossroads and either follow the passage ahead to the north (turn to **366**), or turn to the west (turn to **11**).

278

The passageway soon comes to an end at a locked wooden door. You listen at the door but hear nothing. Will you try to charge the door down? If so, turn to **156**. If you would rather turn round and go back to the junction, turn to **92**.

279

The creature you are facing is a VAMPIRE! You have various lines of attack. Your sword will do little real damage. A Crucifix will hold him at bay but will not kill him. If you have either of these you may use it to get you through the west door (turn to **380**). If you are determined to kill the Vampire, you must overpower it and drive a wooden stake through its heart. If you have a wooden stake and wish to try to kill the Vampire, turn to **17**. If you have none of these, draw your sword and turn to **333**.

280

You arrive back at the junction and this time take the passageway to the east. The passageway runs for several paces eastwards, then turns north. Turn to **311**.

281

The narrow passageway eventually becomes too small for you to walk along. You get down on your hands and knees, and crawl. Eventually, you will get no further and there seems to be no way through, so you decide to return to the main passage. You head for the junction. Turn to **10**.

282

The four creatures shuffling towards you are mindless ZOMBIES. Their vacant eyes suggest that their actions are controlled by a will which is not their own. You are still too dizzy to think properly, but you must act quickly. The first Zombie reaches you and prepares to swing his club. You must fight him.

ZOMBIE   *SKILL* 7   *STAMINA* 6

If you defeat the first Zombie, add 2 *LUCK* points and turn to face the other three (fight each in turn):

	SKILL	*STAMINA*
ZOMBIE with scythe	6	6
ZOMBIE with pick	6	6
ZOMBIE with axe	6	5

If you defeat all four, turn to **115**.

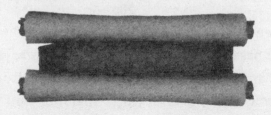

283

You arrive back at the junction and progress westwards. Turn to **251**.

284

'You again?' says the Mazemaster, obviously annoyed at being disturbed. 'You are disturbing my concentration. Be off with you!' You begin to explain that you only returned by mistake, but as you open your mouth, an icy glare from the old man silences you. You decide to leave him to it. To leave by the west door, turn to **46**. To leave by the south door, turn to **392**.

285

You see a well-used door on the right-hand (east) side of the passageway. With your ear to the keyhole, you listen and hear a man screaming for help from inside. Will you open the door (turn to **213**) or walk on (turn to **314**)?

286

The narrow staircase is cut into the rock and there are about twenty steps leading down. At the bottom of the steps a passageway leads you into a large open chamber. This chamber stinks of putrefying flesh. The smell is so bad that you are tempted to turn back. Three bodies lie in the chamber. You may either search the bodies, or tiptoe quietly through the room. What will you do:

Search the first body?	Turn to **294**
Search the second body?	Turn to **275**
Search the third body?	Turn to **148**
Tiptoe through the room?	Turn to **107**

287

The passage continues for quite some time, then you reach the foot of a staircase cut into the rock. You ascend the stairs and they end at a wooden door with rusty hinges. Listening at the door, you can hear some scratching sounds. You try the handle and the door creaks open. You step into a bare room scattered with bones. There is a door on the wall opposite. Gnawing at the bones are three GIANT RATS which stop to look at you as you enter. Each is at least one metre long and their tatty coats indicate that they are fighters. You will have to take them on if you are going to get through the room, as they no doubt see you as a tasty meal. If you have collected any Cheese during your adventure, turn to **32**. Otherwise, turn to **309**.

288

Turn to **182**.

289

You look frantically round the room but can see nothing to aid you. Suddenly your eyes stop on the pack of cards he was fingering as you entered, and you remember the rumours and stories the villagers told you: 'The Warlock's power comes from his cards.' The sorcerer sees your interest in them and you both rush for the table. You get there first. 'Leave those alone,' he screams, 'or you risk my fullest wrath!' But you move backwards and set fire to one with your lantern. He cries out wildly and then begins to plead with you to leave them alone. One by one you burn the cards and, as you do so, the Warlock diminishes in stature. As the last card goes up in flames, he stands facing you, a broken man. 'My book!' he croaks, and he tries to unlock the door on the far side. You race across to him with your sword drawn and spring at him. Resolve this battle:

WARLOCK *SKILL 7* *STAMINA 12*

If you win, turn to **396**.

290

Turn to **198**.

291

You are standing in the middle of an east-west corridor. To the east is a dead end, which you can investigate by turning to **315**. To the west is a familiar junction. To go this way turn to **52**. Another passageway – quite a short one – leads off to the north and ends in a large wooden door. If you wish to try the door, turn to **227**.

292

Northwards the passageway ends at a solid wooden door. You listen at the door but can hear nothing. There appears to be no choice but to open the door and enter the room, which you do. It's a large, square room. You flash your lantern around the room and catch a quick glimpse of its emptiness – although there are murals on the wall – before your lantern suddenly goes out. You try to re-light it, but it will not catch. In the blackness you hear a succession of frightful noises. Howls, screams, cries and wails are getting louder and louder until they reach the pitch where you must cover your ears. Do you have a Blue Candle? If so, turn to **239**. If not, turn to **40**.

293

You arrive back at the junction in the passage and walk straight on eastwards. Turn to **113**.

294

You find 5 Gold Pieces in the pockets of the corpse. Enter these on your *Adventure Sheet* and add *1 LUCK* point for your find. You may now either:

Search the second body	Turn to **275**
Search the third body	Turn to **148**
Tiptoe through the room northwards	Turn to **107**

295

You find no secret passages. However, your explorations attract some sort of creature, and as you listen you can hear something coming down the corridor towards you.

To find out what sort of wandering monster you have come across, turn to **161**. You must fight the creature and, if you defeat it, you may press on down the passageway by turning to **48**. However, at section **161** you will not be told where to progress to, so write down '**48**' now so you will know where to go after **161**.

296

The box contains a small leather-bound book entitled *The Making and Casting of Dragonfire*. You open the pages and begin to read. Fortunately it is written in your own language and so was probably not understood by the Orcs – otherwise this treasure would certainly not be as loosely guarded as it was.

The book is written in tiny handwriting by Farrigo Di Maggio. In it he tells the story of his life's work; the creation of the Dragonfire spell with which to fight evil Dragons. You read how, in his last years, Farrigo finally perfected his spell but by then was too old to make use of it. So he completed his book, locked it in a chest and hid it in the depths of Firetop Mountain, afraid that it might fall into the wrong hands. The last page reads:

> AND SO, YOU WHO NOW HOLD THIS BOOK, YOU
> HAVE MY LIFE'S WORK IN YOUR HANDS. THE
> POWER OF DESTRUCTION IS YOURS IF YOU WISH
> IT, BUT DO NOT WASTE IT. UNLESS YOU USE THE
> SPELL FOR THE PURPOSE FOR WHICH IT WAS
> INTENDED, YOU SHALL BE CONSUMED BY EVIL
> ITSELF AND DIE BY THE FIRE FROM YOUR OWN
> HANDS. REMEMBER, ONLY WHEN THE DRAGON
> BREATHES ITS FIRE AT YOU SHOULD YOU RAISE
> YOUR ARMS AND SAY:
>
> EKIL ERIF
> EKAM ERIF
> ERIF ERIF
> DI MAGGIO'

You say these words slowly and softly. Suddenly the pages seem to glow and as this glow disappears, so do the words on the pages of the book. You repeat the spell to yourself to memorize it and leave the room. Turn to **42**.

297

You are in an east-west corridor with a T-junction at both ends. To go westwards, turn to **150**. To go eastwards, turn to **256**.

298

The bridge is slippery from the splashings of the water. At one point you slip on a tuft of wet moss covering the timbers. Roll one die. A roll of 6 means you slip from the bridge into the water below and start swimming for the nearest bank – turn to **86**. Any other roll is lucky; you managed to hold on and you reach the north bank (turn to **7**).

299

The passageway runs east for several metres and then runs north. You walk a long way northwards. You may check for secret passages along the way (turn to **260**) or simply proceed northwards (turn to **359**).

300

On the east wall of the passage you see another door, this time made of solid metal. Listening at the door you hear the sound of tortured screams coming from within. If you wish to try opening the door, turn to **102**. If you decide to ignore this room and continue up the corridor, turn to **303**.

301

To your left, on the west face of the passage, there is a rough-cut wooden door. You listen at the door and can hear a rasping sound which may be some sort of creature snoring. Do you want to open the door? If so, turn to **82**. If you wish to press on northwards, turn to **208**.

302

Turn to **198**.

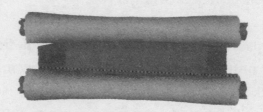

303

You arrive at the end of the passage, where it meets another going east-west. But an iron portcullis blocks your way and no amount of charging is going to budge it. On the wall to your right are two levers and it seems likely that these levers have something to do with raising the portcullis. Do you wish to pull the right lever or the left lever?

Right	Turn to **128**
Left	Turn to **243**

304

The old man is furious at your killing his dog! His eyes turn white with anger. He slowly rises from his seat and as he stands he appears to gain in size and stature. He is changing in front of your eyes. He sprouts hair on his face and forearms. His nose lengthens and becomes dog-like. His teeth are pointed. He is a WEREWOLF and he advances towards you.

You can *Escape* only through the door behind you to the south (turn to **66**). Otherwise you must fight him:

WEREWOLF   *SKILL 8*   *STAMINA 8*

If you defeat him, turn to **203**.

305

Test your Luck three times. If you are Lucky each time, you make it across to the far door and can leave the room. Turn to **162**. On the first throw that you are Unlucky, you step on a hand tile – turn to **108**.

306

You still find no secret passageways. But coming towards you down the corridor you can see a creature-like shape. To find out what is coming towards you, turn to **161** and prepare to fight.

If you kill the creature you encounter, you can go back along the corridor. Turn to **291**. Write down this number so you know where to return to.

307

The passage twists and turns and eventually ends in a solid iron door. You listen but hear nothing. You can try to open the door (turn to **134**) or you can go back to the junction (turn to **87**).

308

You are standing at a crossroads. To the west the passageway goes on a few metres and turns northwards. To the north the passageway ends at a door. To the east the passage continues and eventually turns southwards. Looking south, the passage goes on as far as you can see.

To go west	Turn to **187**
To go north	Turn to **54**
To go south	Turn to **160**
To go east	Turn to **354**

309

You draw your sword and wait for the Rats to spring. As the leader prepares to jump, you shout loudly and leap forward at it. Your cry frightens off the other two and they scamper back a few paces. Fight each of the Rats in turn:

	SKILL	STAMINA
First RAT	5	4
Second RAT	6	3
Third RAT	5	5

If you win, you may leave through the door in the north wall. Turn to **124**.

310

Something is not quite right. You landed a fair blow on him, but he appears not to have noticed the wound! You deduce that this Undead creature is not vulnerable to normal weapons. You may choose a new weapon. Armed with this, or your old weapon, turn to **211**.

311

The passageway ends in a door at which you listen but hear nothing. Trying the handle, you find that the door opens to reveal a large, square room. The room is completely bare, but the floor is covered in a mosaic of tiles. Two shapes stand out on the floor; star-shaped tiles and hand-shaped tiles. A door on the opposite wall is the only way through. Will you:

Walk across the room to the door?	Turn to **305**
Walk across the room stepping only on stars?	Turn to **178**
Walk across the room stepping only on hands?	Turn to **108**

312

You follow a long, narrow passageway which goes north, then west, then north again and you eventually find yourself at a crossroads. Turn to **308**.

313

You check over the body. The poor wretch was obviously caught in the same way that you were, but his weaker skull shattered under the club's blow. He wears a suit of leather armour no better than your own, holds a wooden shield on one wrist and clutches a steel bladed sword in his other hand. In his pockets are 8 Gold Pieces and around his neck is a silver crucifix.

You may take any two of these items you wish. Write them on your Equipment List and turn to **221**. Also add 1 *LUCK* and 1 *SKILL* point.

314

Further up the passage you see a door in the east wall. You listen hard, but can hear no sound. Do you want to open the door to investigate? If so turn to **223**. If you want to walk further up the passage, turn to **300**.

315

The dead-end appears to have no secret passageways, but you can check by turning to **306**. If you don't want to double-check for secret passages, turn to **291**.

316

The water is icy cold. You start to swim and notice that your splashings are attracting a moving 'turbulence' in the water. Will your strength and stamina hold out? Roll two dice. If the roll is equal to or less than your *STAMINA* score, you believe you can make it and swim furiously for the north bank – turn to **151**. If the roll totals more than your *STAMINA* score, you decide not to risk it and return to the south bank – turn to **218**. You may eat Provisions on the south bank.

317

You cut down the Dwarf. He is, as you guessed, dead. Going through the pockets of the two Goblins, you find a large piece of sweet-smelling Cheese. If you wish to take this with you, put it in your pack and leave the room northwards. Turn to **303**.

318

The passageway ends in a dead end. You may either return to the crossroads (turn to **85**) or search for secret passageways (turn to **228**).

319

To find the secret of the second item you have collected, turn to **221** and investigate. If you have already investigated both items, turn to **81**.

320

You run out of the room and slam the door shut behind you. You turn northwards up the passageway passing a similar-looking door further up. Turn to **363**.

321

Turn to **169**.

322

The drawers are all full of nails, tacks and miscellaneous bits and pieces. In one drawer is a copper-coloured key, inscribed with the number *66* which looks interesting. You may keep this key if you discard one item of equipment you are carrying. Adjust your Equipment on your *Adventure Sheet* if you want to take the key. The noise from the north gets louder. You go to the north door to investigate. Turn to **96**.

323

After a few metres you reach another three-way junction. You may go either northwards (turn to **8**) or eastwards (turn to **255**).

324

As you burst through the door, the old man turns to look at you, not in the least perturbed by your intrusion. Suddenly he vanishes! He reappears against the wall and, as you spin round to see him, he laughs. Not the feeble cackle of an old man, but the booming laugh of a much younger man. Again he disappears, and reappears in another corner of the room, glaring at you and taunting you with his evil laugh. You swirl round just in time to see him disappear again. This time he reappears in the air above you and slowly floats down to you. His glaring eyes make you shiver as they approach. Turn to **358**.

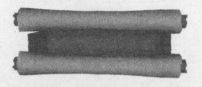

325

You place the helmet on your head. It fits well. A glow begins to fill your body and you seem to possess a power and confidence beyond anything you have felt before. The helmet is blessed with magic and will allow you to add 1 point to all future dice rolls when computing your own Attack Strength during combat so long as you wear it. Note this on your Equipment List and return to the junction (turn to **87**).

326

You enter a small room with bare, rocky walls. On the far wall hangs a golden key. There appears to be no way through the room. Do you want to go for the key (turn to **35**) or leave it and return to the junction (turn to **229**)?

327

The body on the floor turns visibly older in front of your eyes. The face looks fifty, then ninety, then well over a hundred years old. The skin rots and the eyes decompose as you watch. You notice a movement coming from the creature's chest. As the remnants of the Vampire decay, a small black face breaks through its chest. It resembles a small black shrew, but as it frees itself and unfurls its wings you realize it is a bat. You lunge at it, but it flaps away into the darkness.

You search the whole chamber quickly (remember, there are several other coffins there!) and find 30 Gold Pieces, a book, and a Y-shaped stick. You may take these items (enter them on your *Adventure Sheet*) if you will leave behind one item of Equipment you are already carrying.

You can leave through the west door. Turn to **380**. If you are hungry you may take Provisions here, and you can add 3 *LUCK* points for defeating the Vampire.

328

Both pieces of wood are Y-shaped and smooth, as if washed up from a river. You may put these in your pack and then either leave through the north door (turn to **73**) or stay and examine the rope (turn to **125**). If you take the pieces of wood, you must leave behind one item from your pack.

329

You set off and find yourself in the middle of a north–south passageway. There is a door in the western wall of the passage. Opposite the door is a passage going off eastwards. To the north you can see a door some metres ahead. To the south you can see a junction. Which will you choose:

The door in the west wall?	Turn to **157**
The door to the north?	Turn to **392**
Eastwards?	Turn to **299**
Southwards?	Turn to **238**

330

The barrels contain a clear brown liquid. You sniff it. It smells like rum. You taste it. It *is* rum. You cup your hands, pour some in and take a swig. You gasp – by golly, it's good! Restore 6 points of *STAMINA* and 1 *LUCK*. Turn to **81**.

331

The creature is man-sized but its long arms look very powerful. Resolve this battle:

TROLL   *SKILL 8*   *STAMINA 8*

If you win, you may head northwards (turn to **287**).

332

You find yourself at a door blocking the east end of an east–west passage. To go through the door, turn to **329**. Looking westwards, the passage turns to the north. To go this way, turn to **4**.

333

As you swing your sword at the creature, it reaches out and catches the blade in its hand! Your weapon is almost ineffective against the considerable strength of the creature. You realize this and panic, but you must fight on.

VAMPIRE   *SKILL 10*   *STAMINA 10*

If you defeat the Vampire, turn to **327**. If you wish to try to *Escape*, which you may only do after 6 full Attack Rounds, you will have to be lucky. *Test your Luck*. If you are Lucky, you may *Escape* through the west door (turn to **380**). If you are Unlucky, you must continue this fight for a further 6 Attack Rounds before trying to *Escape* again. If you roll an 11 or 12 and you are Unlucky (i.e. your current *LUCK* score is below 11), then turn to **224**.

334

As you speak the old man rises to his feet. 'Oh my, oh my, a stranger!' he starts. 'Well, do come in, the shop is open. What can I get you? What would you like to buy? What takes your fancy? Which way are you headed? North? Well?' You tell the old man your story. He listens intently and replies, 'Oh yes, in that case you will undoubtedly need one of my Blue Candles. That will be 20 Gold Pieces please. Cash if you don't mind. Yes, I know it's expensive, but isn't everything these days? Not so long ago these were only 5 Gold Pieces each; but you know what has happened to the price of candlewax since the Long Dark Night – oh, but you probably don't since you don't come from these parts. Never mind. I can guarantee if s still worth the price. You might need it sooner than you think . . .'

If you decide to buy a candle, pay for it and add it to your Equipment List. You are getting a little tired of his constant prattling. Leave the room and go northwards. Turn to **292**.

335

Turn to **182**.

336

You are in a small, foul-smelling room. You notice two doors: one to the west and one behind you to the south. The furniture in the room is sparse and has been made mostly from bits of old boats. There appears to be nothing of value in the room, but a bunch of keys hangs on the wall. An old man in ragged clothes is slumped asleep on a 'bench' made from half a rowing boat, snoring loudly. Next to him is a vicious-looking brown dog with red eyes and black teeth, whom you have awakened and who now is eyeing you suspiciously. A deep growl is coming from its throat. You may:

Tiptoe an exit through the south door	Turn to **66**
Bang on the door behind you and cough a few 'Ahem's' to wake up the old man	Turn to **172**
Leap across the room with sword drawn to cut down the dog	Turn to **249**

337

You find no secret passages, but as you press the walls, you hear a click. You feel dizzy and slump to the ground. When you come to, the surroundings look strange. Turn to **267**.

338

You approach the statue cautiously. A scampering behind you makes you flash round ... but it is only a rat. You feel at the jewel, but it is solidly in place. You try to work your sword in behind it and as you work, you hear an ominous creaking noise. To your horror the statue is beginning to move! You jump down and draw your sword. The IRON CYCLOPS cranes its head round towards you and steps down from its pedestal. You must fight!

IRON CYCLOPS   SKILL 10   STAMINA 10

If you win, turn to **75**. If you want to *Escape* during combat, you can run through the door back to the junction. Turn to **93**.

339

The lock was obviously inadequate; it flies off and lands on the floor several metres away. You lift up the heavy lid and your eyes widen as you see the gold sheen coming from within. A fair number of Gold Pieces are inside. In one corner lies a small black bottle with a tight glass stopper, containing a liquid of some kind. Also in the chest is a silky black glove. But as you are admiring this treasure you hear a soft click and wince in pain as a small dart shoots forward into your stomach. Roll one die and subtract this number of points from your *STAMINA* to determine the effect of the poison on the dart tip. If you are still alive, turn to **201**.

340

You try various items of equipment against the gaze of the painting, but none seems to work. You may try any of the following if you have them:

Slash the painting with your sword	Turn to **388**
Hold a jewel up in front of it	Turn to **31**
Plunge a wooden stake into it	Turn to **241**
Throw cheese at it	Turn to **45**

341

The old man glares at you as you enter the room. You may either apologize, explain that you lost your way and leave through either the door in the west (turn to **46**) or south (turn to **392**) walls, or alternatively you may try to talk to the old man. If you want to talk to him, you can either be pleasant (turn to **220**) or you can *demand* that he answers your questions (turn to **191**).

342

The Wererat slumps to the ground. You search his body and find 2 Gold Pieces, his fare from the last crossing. You curse him for trying to overcharge you. Add the 2 Gold Pieces to your Gold and row yourself across the river. Add 2 *LUCK* points. As you moor the boat on the north bank you look back at the body. It has vanished! Turn to **7**.

343

The door bursts open and you fall headlong into a room. But your heart jumps as you realize you are not landing on the floor, but plunging down a pit of some kind! Luckily the pit is not particularly deep and you land in a heap less than two metres down. Lose 1 *STAMINA* point for your bruises, climb out of the pit into the room and leave through the door, heading westwards. Turn to **92**.

344

You sheathe your sword and walk up to the water. Is it safe to swim? Although you cannot see any immediate signs of danger either in the water or around its banks, there is no way through on the north side of the river. You suddenly notice a gleaming sword lying on the river bed several steps in. You wade in to retrieve it. It is light in your hand, far less cumbersome than your own weapon, and it has a keen edge. This marvellous weapon will add 1 point to your *SKILL* whilst you use it. Note this on your Equipment List. A mysterious voice speaking directly to your mind seems to be telling you to throw your own sword into the river. Will you? If so, turn to **56**. If you want to keep both swords, turn to **153**.

345

You follow the passage eastwards for several metres, then it turns to the north. Shortly you reach another junction where you may either go straight on (turn to **381**) or you may turn right, into an eastwards passage that soon turns north (turn to **311**).

346

The luck of the cards may or may not be with you. You have two choices.

You may leave all luck to the cards. Throw two dice. If the number is even, then you lose this number of Gold Pieces or all your Gold if you don't have enough. If the number is odd, then you win this number of Gold Pieces.

Alternatively, you may use your *LUCK* to help you win. *Test your Luck.* If you are Lucky, throw two dice to see how many Gold Pieces you win. If you are Unlucky, throw two dice to see how many Gold Pieces you lose.

Make the appropriate alterations on your *Adventure Sheet*. If you won, you may add 2 *LUCK* points for your good fortune. When this is done, turn to **131**.

A Troll emerges from its chamber

347

Turn to **182**.

348

You are in a pit, a little bruised but not too seriously hurt. You look around as you get back on your feet and can see two passageways: a short one to the south which opens into a small chamber, and another heading northwards. You are a little worried about the crash your fall has made, and even more by the gruntings you can hear coming from the chamber to the south. Before you can collect your thoughts, a large, ugly head pokes around the corner and a TROLL emerges from its chamber. Your ankle is twisted and you cannot move quickly, but the Troll is ready for a fight. You will have to face the brute. Turn to **331** – but if you have a Potion of Invisibility, turn to **51**.

349

You walk a few metres down the passage and find yourself at a dead end. You may either return to the crossroads (turn to **267**) or investigate the end of the passage (turn to **30**).

350

As the 'turbulence' surrounds you, you can feel the jostlings of many small fish. They start ripping your flesh with vicious bites and you realize that you are surrounded by deadly PIRANHAS!

If, during your struggle with the Crocodile, you have wounded it, you are lucky and most of the fish attack the bleeding reptile. If you have not wounded the Crocodile, then the fish may go for either you or it. Throw one die. If you throw a 1 or 2, the majority of the Piranhas go for you. If you throw a 3–6, the majority attack the Crocodile.

Treat the Piranhas as a single creature. If, as a result of the above, the *majority* of the fish attack you, their scores are:

PIRANHAS   SKILL 5   STAMINA 5

If, as a result of the above, the majority attack the Crocodile and the *remainder* attack you, they have:

PIRANHAS   SKILL 5   STAMINA 1

If you win you can swim to shore. Turn to **7**. You may eat Provisions here – and restore 1 *LUCK* point.

351

You arrive back at the junction and turn eastwards. Turn to **76**.

352

As you approach you feel his eyes burn into you with considerable power. You begin to weaken under his gaze. Lose 1 *STAMINA* point. You are gradually losing your own will. Will you try to draw your sword and fight him (turn to **74**) or look for some other means of attack in your bag (turn to **279**)?

353

You lunge at the old man as he leaps towards you with outstretched arms – and run him through the chest with your sword. You curse as you realize that he was making no attempt to attack you; his wild excitement must merely have been relief after having been imprisoned for what had apparently been a very long time. You will now get no information out of him on the perils of the adventure ahead. Turn to **314** to progress up the passageway.

354

You are standing at a bend in the passage where you may go either west or south.

To go west	Turn to **308**
To go south	Turn to **52**
If you want to check for secret passages on the way westwards	Turn to **14**
If you want to check for secret passages as you go south	Turn to **234**

355

You grope along the wall but can find no way of escape. The noise is causing you to scream in pain! Subtract 1 *SKILL* point. You may try either the east wall (turn to **181**) or the north wall (turn to **265**).

356

The old man looks at you, accepts your greetings and bids you sit down. You sit at the table and notice that he is glaring at you. His piercing stare is becoming hypnotic, but you realize this and break eye contact. He opens his mouth to speak and to your amazement, instead of an old man's voice, the whole room resonates to a powerful voice which seems to be coming from the walls themselves. You throw a glance back at the man and can see him changing before your very eyes. He is of imposing height. His tattered old rags have become robes of velvet and gold. His black eyes are fixed directly on yours. He has been expecting you . . .

Turn to **358**.

357

The passage runs for some distance northwards and then starts to open into a large cavern with rough walls. There appears to be no way through. Will you return to the junction (turn to **269**) or enter the cavern (turn to **57**)?

Your adversary now stands at the far end of the room

358

The battle will call upon all your reserves of strength and cunning. Your adversary has disappeared, and now stands at the far end of the room in front of a door with two locks. How will you approach him:

Grip your sword firmly and advance towards him?	Turn to **142**
Look through your pack for a weapon to use?	Turn to **105**
Look around the room for another means of attack or defence?	Turn to **389**

359

You are at a crossroads.

To go north	Turn to **190**
To go south	Turn to **94**
To go east	Turn to **121**
To go west	Turn to **385**

360

The door slams shut with a loud bang behind you. You find yourself in a passageway running ahead northwards. You follow it for several metres, until it bends to the west, and continue onwards. Some way down the passage you come across a narrow opening in the north wall and decide to go through. Turn to **89**.

361

You snatch the key from its hook. It has the number *125* inscribed on it. But your lungs are bursting. Roll two dice. If the number is less than or equal to your *SKILL* score, you make it across the room to the door (turn to **136**). If it exceeds your *SKILL* score, you are forced to take a breath of poison gas. Reduce your *SKILL* score by 2 and your *STAMINA* score by 3 and dash for the door (turn to **136**).

362

As you try the walls up the passageway, a secret door opens up along the west wall. Turn to **177**.

363

Further up the passage on the west wall you see another similar door. You listen at the door and grimace to hear the worst singing you have ever heard in your life! Do you want to go into the room to investigate this hideous din (turn to **370**) or walk on up the passageway (turn to **42**)?

364

As you push the knob, a small stone doorway slides

open. You can either ignore it and return to the junction (turn to **256**) or you can climb through (turn to **373**). You must make your decision quickly, as the door shuts of its own accord in a minute's time.

365

The Orcs attack you one at a time.

	SKILL	STAMINA
First ORC	6	4
Second ORC	5	3
Third ORC	6	4
Fourth ORC	5	2
Fifth ORC	4	4

If you win, turn to **183**. If you wish to *Escape* during the battle (don't forget your penalty for this), turn to **237**.

366

You are following a passageway which leads ahead to the north. After several metres it bends sharply to the east. You continue eastwards until you eventually come across a narrow opening in the north wall. You may go through this opening (turn to **89**) or continue eastwards (turn to **62**).

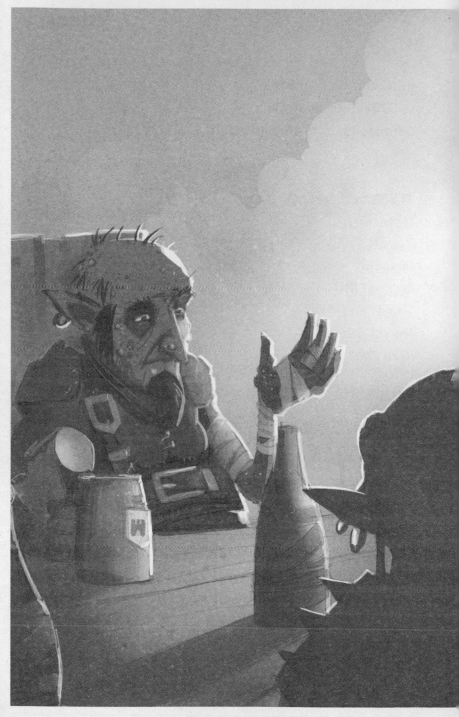

Seated around the table are two small creatures with warty skin

367

You arrive at another junction in the passageway. If you would like to turn westwards, turn to **235**. If you wish to go east, turn to **323**.

368

The Warlock's laugh resonates in his chamber. 'We will see which of us is the mouse!' he cries, and he holds his hand in the air. As he snaps his fingers, a blue flame streams from his hand at you. Lose 3 *STAMINA* points. You will have to try something else:

Draw your sword and advance	Turn to **142**
Try something else from your rucksack	Turn to **105**

369

You swallow some of the liquid (turn to **109**).

370

The door opens to reveal a small room. The room is dirty and unkempt. A straw mattress lies in one corner. In the centre of the room is a wooden table upon which a candle burns, lighting the room with its flickering flame. A small box rests under the table. Seated around the table are two small creatures with warty skin, dressed in leather armour. They are drinking some sort of grog and, by the way they stagger to their feet on your arrival, you assume they are very drunk. You may either draw your sword and leap forward at them (turn to **116**) or slam the door quickly and run on up the passage (turn to **42**).

371

Safe for the moment, you investigate the cavern and find a passageway which continues to the west. Turn to **274**. You may rest and eat Provisions before you continue, and add 3 *LUCK* points for defeating the Dragon.

372

The battle commences!

	SKILL	STAMINA
ORC CHIEFTAIN	7	6
SERVANT	5	3

Fight them one at a time. If you defeat them both, turn to **21**.

373

You are at the south end of a north–south passageway – at a dead end. If you go northwards you will reach a crossroads. Turn to **85**.

374

The Skeletons do not notice you and disappear through the door into the Boat House. Breathing a sigh of relief, you press on to try the door at the north end of the passage. But before you go, you may eat some Provisions and you may add 2 *LUCK* points for evading the Skeletons. Turn to **207**.

375

You arrive back at the junction and this time turn northwards. Turn to **5**.

376

You may collect all the copper pieces on the table. They are worth a total of 4 Gold Pieces. Then you can leave through the door. Turn to **291**. You may pause to eat Provisions, and you may add 3 *LUCK* points.

377

As you draw your sword, the WINGED GREMLIN flaps into the air and attacks you, while the old man rushes over to the bookshelf, touches a book and escapes through a secret doorway that opens for him. But you must fight his pet.

WINGED GREMLIN   SKILL 5   STAMINA 7

If you beat the Gremlin, turn to **196**.

378

You wipe your bloodied sword on the mattress. The green blood leaves a slimy stain on the straw. Stepping over the bodies towards the table you flinch at the foul stench of the creatures. You pick up the box from under the table and examine it. It is a small wooden box with crude hinges. The name 'Farrigo Di Maggio' is inscribed on a brass nameplate on its lid. If you wish to open the box, turn to **296**. If you decide to leave it behind and leave the room, turn to **42**.

379

As you prepare to strike the box, the rumbling sound gets louder. You lift your sword high and prepare to strike. As your blade comes down on the box, a loud crack deafens you and, from one corner of the room, a small bolt of lightning darts through the air to the sword hilt, sending you reeling across the room.

Test your luck. If you are Lucky, your sword has shattered and lies on the floor, but you managed to release your grip just before the lightning struck. If you are Unlucky, your charred remains have formed a small black outline on the floor. Next time, do not try to strike the chest! If you were Lucky, you may try to use keys from your rucksack. Turn to **139**.

380

You are in a narrow east–west corridor. Looking westwards you can see a crossroads ahead. You go on to the crossroads. Turn to **37**.

381

The passage ends at a wooden door, trimmed in iron. Various inscriptions adorn the door, but none makes any sense to you. You listen, but hear nothing. You may either open the door (turn to **84**) or return to the junction (turn to **280**).

382

You hold the Eye up in front of him and the jewel gives off a dull glow. You point it towards him and he shrieks! He backs away into a corner and a beam of light shoots from the jewel. As it falls on him he sinks to the floor and a remarkable transformation takes place. He starts to shrivel and grow visibly old in front of you. His skin wrinkles and cracks and he slowly becomes an amorphous heap in the corner. After some moments, the jewel stops glowing and you approach the lifeless bundle of cloth; his robes are all that remain. Turn to **396**.

You can see a number of Skeleton-men

383

A sign above the door reads 'Boat House'. The door is firmly locked but a small barred window allows you to look inside. You can see a number of Skeleton-men working on building a boat of some sort. They move in a series of quick, jerky actions, rather insect-like.

If you have a key clearly labelled 'Boat House'	Turn to **80**.
If you want to try to break the door down	Turn to **264**.
If you want to return to the riverbank and try another route	Turn to **129**.

384

The door opens into a passage which you follow northwards. Shortly you reach a bend and follow it round to the east. Several metres on, you reach a junction at which you may either go north (turn to **262**) or continue eastwards (turn to **307**).

385

You travel westwards for several paces, then the passage turns to the north. Some way up, you reach a junction. You may go south (turn to **114**) or west (turn to **297**). To the north, the passage ends shortly at a dead end. If you wish to go up here, turn to **398**.

386

You climb on the raft and start to punt your way across the river. The going is not easy. In the middle of the river the raft seems to take on a will of its own and bobs up and down dangerously. You realize it is attempting to capsize itself and throw you into the river! You may either trust your strength and luck to hold on and keep punting to the north side (turn to **55**) or jump into the water and attempt to swim back to the south bank (turn to **166**).

387

You try the keys. Not one will turn. As you try to turn the third key, small catches drop and your last memory is a sting of pain as three small darts pierce your skin. Each is treated with a quick-acting poison.

Remember not to use this combination of keys next time!

388

Your sword flies out of your hand, into the air and you must leap aside as it comes down on you. It grazes your cheek as it falls. Lose *1 STAMINA* point. You decide you'd better leave the room. Pick up your sword and turn to **90**. Lose 1 more *SKILL* point in fear of the Warlock's power.

389

Test your Luck. If you are Lucky, turn to **289**. If you are Unlucky, turn to **112**.

390

The Ghoul twitches and dies at your feet. You search its body and find little of interest. A couple of earrings, worth 1 Gold Piece between them, are in one of its pockets. You may take these. If you haven't already searched the first body, you do so and find 5 Gold Pieces, which you may also take. You may also stop here, rest and eat Provisions. You can add 2 *LUCK* points for killing the Ghoul. Now you may either press on northwards (turn to **120**) or search the second body (turn to **393**).

391

You are at the south end of a north–south corridor. Looking northwards, you can see a passage coming off from the east wall. Do you want:

To go up to this passage?	Turn to **52**
To check for secret passages as you walk northwards?	Turn to **362**
To go south, following a bend to the west?	Turn to **48**

Several metres away is a Giant Spider

392

You are in a north–south corridor. You may go either northwards through a large wooden door (turn to **206**) or south (turn to **329**).

393

You search the pockets of the other body and find 8 Gold Pieces, a bottle of liquid and an old piece of parchment. You may take these items. To read the parchment, turn to **212**. To test the liquid, turn to **369**.

394

The boots are well-fashioned in a deep red leather. They are much sturdier than your own and fit you well. You try a few steps but are horrified to find that you cannot move, and the boots seem to be gripping your feet with considerable force. As you struggle to free yourself, you hear a crack and a smash as a stalactite falls from the roof; you crane round to see a large black shape shifting towards you. As it approaches, you turn cold. Several metres away is a GIANT SPIDER, at least a metre across, advancing towards you on spiny legs, mandibles clicking nervously in anticipation of its next meal. You draw your sword to defend yourself as it stalks you. You cannot move and thus must subtract 2 from each dice roll you make to calculate your Attack Strength.

GIANT SPIDER   *SKILL 7*   *STAMINA 8*

If you win the battle, turn to **232**.

395

You step over the bones on the floor to take a closer look at the Boat House. You pick up and study a few of the tools scattered around: hammers, nails, chisels and the like, but they appear very ordinary. You hear a banging sound coming from beyond the north door and have time for one further search before you must react. Do you look through the drawers of the benches around the room (turn to **322**) or check the tools more carefully (turn to **34**)?

396

With the Warlock now defeated, you know your quest is almost over. You approach the door with two locks. There are no keys around. You retrieve two keys from your pack and try them in the locks. They turn! You open the door and peer round. Turn to **242**. If you have no keys, you may try to break down the door, and this you will do at the cost of almost all your *STAMINA*. Reduce your *STAMINA* by 5 and enter the room. Turn to **242**.

397

The door opens to reveal a small room with a stone floor and dirty walls. There is a stale smell in the air. In the centre of the room is a makeshift wooden table on which is standing a lit candle. Under the table is a small box. In the far corner of the room is a straw mattress. You may either open the box (turn to **240**) or leave the room (turn to **363**).

398

You feel around the rock face at the end of the passage. One rock comes free and reveals a small knob with a handle on the end. Will you push it (turn to **364**) or pull it (turn to **12**)?

399

The current is strong and takes you swiftly downstream. You are washed along through a narrow opening and out into a large cavern with banks on both sides. The current washes you on to the south bank. Turn to **218**.

400
YOUR QUEST IS OVER

The Warlock of Firetop Mountain is no more and you are now the owner of the Sorcerer's riches. At least a thousand Gold Pieces, jewellery, diamonds, rubies and pearls are in the chest. Hidden under these you find the Warlock's spell book and as you leaf through the pages, you realize that this tome is probably more valuable than all the treasure. Instructions are given for the control of all the secrets – and the creatures – of Firetop Mountain. With this book, unlimited power is yours and the safety of your return to the village is ensured. Or, if you would prefer, you could remain as master of the domain of Firetop Mountain . .

HOW TO FIGHT
THE CREATURES OF
THE UNDERWORLD

Before embarking on your adventure, you must first determine your own strengths and weaknesses by rolling dice to determine your initial scores. On pages 206–207 there is an *Adventure Sheet* which you may use to record the details of an adventure. On it you will find boxes for recording your *SKILL*, *STAMINA* and *LUCK* scores. You are advised to either record your scores on the Adventure Sheet in pencil, or make photocopies of the sheet to use in future adventures.

SKILL, STAMINA AND LUCK

To determine your *Initial SKILL, STAMINA* and *LUCK* scores:

- Roll one die. Add 6 to this number and enter this total in the *SKILL* box on the *Adventure Sheet*.
- Roll both dice. Add 12 to the number rolled and enter this total in the *STAMINA* box.
- Roll one die, add 6 to this number and enter this total in the *LUCK* box.

SKILL reflects your swordsmanship and fighting

expertise; the higher the better. *STAMINA* represents your strength; the higher your *STAMINA,* the longer you will survive. *LUCK* represents how lucky a person you are. Luck – and magic – are facts of life in the fantasy world you are about to explore.

SKILL, STAMINA and *LUCK* scores change constantly during an adventure, so keep an eraser handy. You must keep an accurate record of these scores. But never rub out your *Initial* scores. Although you may receive additional *SKILL, STAMINA* and *LUCK* points, these totals may never exceed your *Initial* scores, except on very rare occasions, when instructed on a particular page.

BATTLES

When you are told to fight a creature, you must resolve the battle as described below. First record the creature's *SKILL* and *STAMINA* scores (as given on the page) in an empty *Monster Encounter Box* on your *Adventure Sheet.* The sequence of combat is then:

1. Roll the two dice for the creature. Add its *SKILL* score. This total is **its** *Attack Strength.*
2. Roll the two dice for yourself. Add your current *SKILL.* This total is **your** *Attack Strength.*
3. Whose *Attack Strength* is higher? If your *Attack Strength* is higher, you have wounded the creature.

If the creature's *Attack Strength* is higher, it has wounded you. (If both are the same, you have both missed – start the next *Attack Round* from step 1 above.)

4. If you wounded the creature, subtract 2 points from **its** *STAMINA* score. You may use *LUCK* here to do additional damage (see 'Using Luck in Battles' below).

5. If the creature wounded you, subtract 2 points from **your** *STAMINA* score. You may use *LUCK* to minimize the damage (see below).

6. Make the appropriate changes to either the creature's or your own *STAMINA* scores (and your *LUCK* score if you used *LUCK*) and begin the next *Attack Round* (repeat steps 1-6).

7. This continues until the *STAMINA* score of either you or the creature you are fighting has been reduced to zero (death).

ESCAPING FROM BATTLES

On some pages you will be given the option of *Escaping from the battle. You may only Escape* if it is offered to you on the page. If you do run away, the creature automatically scores one wound on you (subtract 2 STAMINA points) as you flee. Such is the price of cowardice. You can use LUCK on this wound in the normal way (see 'Using Luck in Battles' below)

LUCK

Sometimes you will be told to *Test your Luck*. As you will discover, using Luck is a risky business. The way you *Test your Luck* is as follows:

Roll two dice. If the number rolled is *equal to* or *less than* your current *LUCK* score, you have been *lucky*. If the number rolled is *higher* than your current *LUCK* score, you have been *unlucky*. The consequences of being *lucky* or *unlucky* will be found on the page. Each time you *Test your Luck,* you must subtract one point from your current *LUCK* score. So the more you rely on luck, the more risky this becomes.

USING LUCK IN BATTLES

In battles, you always have the option of using your luck either to score a more serious wound on a creature, or to minimize the effects of a wound the creature has just scored on you.

IF YOU HAVE JUST WOUNDED THE CREATURE: you may *Test your Luck* as described above. If you are *lucky,* subtract an *extra* 2 points from the creature's *STAMINA* score (i.e. 4 instead of 2 normally). But if you are *unlucky,* you must restore 1 point to the creature's *STAMINA* (so instead of scoring the normal 2 points of damage, you have now scored only 1).

IF THE CREATURE HAS JUST WOUNDED YOU: you can *Test your Luck* to try to minimize the wound. If you are *lucky,* restore 1 point of your *STAMINA* (ie. instead of doing 2 points of damage, it has done only 1). If you are *unlucky,* subtract 1 *extra STAMINA* point.

Don't forget to subtract 1 point from your *LUCK* score each time you *Test your Luck.*

RESTORING SKILL, STAMINA AND LUCK

Occasionally, a page may give instructions to alter your *SKILL* score. A Magic Weapon may increase your *SKILL,* but remember that only one weapon can be used at a time! You cannot claim 2 *SKILL* bonuses for carrying two Magic Swords. Your *SKILL* score can never exceed its *Initial* value unless specifically instructed. Drinking the Potion of Skill (see later) will restore your *SKILL* to its *Initial* level at any time.

STAMINA AND PROVISIONS

Your *STAMINA* score will change a lot during the adventure. As you near your goal, your *STAMINA* level may be dangerously low and battles may be particularly risky, so be careful!

You start the game with enough Provisions for ten meals. A separate *Provisions Remaining* box is provided on the *Adventure Sheet* for recording details of *Provisions*. You may eat only **one** meal at a time. When you eat a meal, add 4 points to your *STAMINA* score and deduct 1 point from your *Provisions*. Remember that you have a long way to go, so use your Provisions wisely!

Don't forget that your *STAMINA* score may never exceed its *Initial* value unless specifically instructed on a page. Drinking the Potion of Strength (see later) will restore your *STAMINA* to its *Initial* level at any time.

LUCK

You will find additions to your *LUCK* score awarded when you have been particularly lucky. Remember that, as with *SKILL* and *STAMINA,* your *LUCK* score may never exceed its *Initial* value unless specifically instructed on a page. Drinking the Potion of Fortune (see later) will restore your *LUCK* to its *Initial* level at any time, and increase your *Initial LUCK* by 1 point.

EQUIPMENT AND POTIONS

You start your adventure with a sword, leather armour, a shield and a backpack containing Provisions for the trip. But you will find lots more items as the adventure unfolds.

You may also take a magical potion which will aid you on your quest. Each bottle of potion contains enough for *one* measure, i.e. it can only be used **once** during an adventure. Choose ONE of the following:

- A Potion of Skill – restores *SKILL* points.
- A Potion of Strength – restores *STAMINA* points.
- A Potion of Fortune – restores *LUCK* points and adds 1 to *Initial LUCK*.

These potions may be taken at any time during the adventure. Taking a measure of potion will restore *SKILL*, *STAMINA* or *LUCK* scores to their *Initial* level. The Potion of Fortune will increase your *Initial LUCK* score by 1 point and restore *LUCK* to this new *Initial* level.

HINTS ON PLAY

There is only one true way through the Warlock's dungeon and it will probably take you several attempts to find it. Make notes and draw a map as you explore – this map will be useful in future adventures and help you to identify unexplored sections of the dungeon.

Not all rooms contain treasure; many merely contain traps and creatures which you will no doubt fall foul of. Several keys are to be found in dungeon rooms. Only by arriving at the Warlock's treasure with the correct keys will you open his chest and get to his treasure.

The 'one true way' involves a minimum of risk and any player, no matter how weak on initial dice rolls, should be able to get through fairly easily.

May the luck of the gods go with you on the adventure!

ADVENTURE SHEET

SKILL

STAMINA

LUCK

EQUIPMENT

GOLD

TREASURE

PROVISIONS

MONSTER ENCOUNTERS

MONSTER:

SKILL =
STAMINA =

MONSTER:

SKILL =
STAMINA =

MONSTER:

SKILL =
STAMINA =

MONSTER:

SKILL =
STAMINA =

MONSTER:

SKILL =
STAMINA =

MONSTER:

SKILL =
STAMINA =

MONSTER:

SKILL =
STAMINA =

MONSTER:

SKILL =
STAMINA =

MONSTER:

SKILL =
STAMINA =

MONSTER:

SKILL =
STAMINA =

MONSTER:

SKILL =
STAMINA =

MONSTER:

SKILL =
STAMINA =

YOU ARE **FIGHTING FANTASY** THE HERO

COLLECT THEM ALL, BRAVE ADVENTURER!

THE WARLOCK OF FIRETOP MOUNTAIN
STEVE JACKSON & IAN LIVINGSTONE

CITY OF THIEVES
IAN LIVINGSTONE

THE CITADEL OF CHAOS
STEVE JACKSON

THE FOREST OF DOOM
IAN LIVINGSTONE

HOUSE OF HELL
STEVE JACKSON

THE PORT OF PERIL
IAN LIVINGSTONE